Inside the Postcard

Inside the Postcard
Working Life at Adie's, Voe

Laureen Johnson

The Shetland Times Ltd.,
Lerwick.
2001

Inside the Postcard: Working Life at Adie's, Voe

Copyright © Laureen Johnson

ISBN 1 898852 78 2

First published by The Shetland Times Ltd, 2001.

Laureen Johnson has asserted her right under the Copyright, Designs and Patents Act 1988, to be identified as author of this work.

All rights reserved.
No part of this publication may be reproduced, stored in a retrieval system, or transmitted, in any form, or by any means, electronic, mechanical, photocopying, recording or otherwise, without the prior written permission of the publishers.

British Library Cataloguing-in-Publication Data.
A catalogue record for this book is available from the British Library.

Cover photographs:
Centre: courtesy of Morag Hay.
Bottom: courtesy of Wilma Couper © Ratter.

Printed and published by
The Shetland Times Ltd.,
Prince Alfred Street,
Lerwick,
Shetland. ZE1 0EP

In memory of Mam and Dad

Contents

Preface xi
Acknowledgements xiii
Introduction xv
Plan of Buildings xvii

Chapter 1	Fishing Days 1	
	Names of Smack Skippers 3	
	The Skipper's Log 6	
	A Smuggling Yarn 11	
	Shoreside Stories 12	
Chapter 2	The Shops, the Slump and the First World War 15	
Chapter 3	The Twenties and Thirties: 19	
	Building up: the 1920s 19	
	The *Ivy*, Multi-Purpose Vessel 22	
	A Sandwick Lass Comes North 25	
	Knitwear - a Changing Scene 26	
	The First Weavers 30	
	Upstairs, Downstairs in Voe House 33	
	Mobile Shop 34	
	Soap, Soda and Sulphur 34	
	The 1930s: Weaving 36	
	The 1930s: "Number Eleven" 37	
	The Carpenters 40	
	On the Road 41	
	Shopping 43	
	Mutton Supply 44	
	Denner Time 45	
	Fitba 45	
	Bright Lights and Batteries .46	
	And so ... The Thirties ended 46	
Chapter 4	Wartime 48	
	The Bakery in Wartime 51	
	A Man's Job? 52	
	Soldiers 54	
	The Lofty Heights of Gonfirth 55	
	At Last 57	

Chapter 5	Post-war	58
	Back to Normality?	58
	The Norwegian Connection	60
	Shop and Office	61
	Tweed - the busiest ever	63
	Picking Shed Lasses	66
	Everest and all that	68
	Fourteen to Five	74
	Emigrants	75
	Outside Wark	77
	Tea, Tourists and Toilets	77
	Dances and Romances	78
	High Days and Holidays	79
	The Queen's Visit	81
	Edward P. Adie	84
	No More Adie's Biscuits	85
	The Later Years	88
	From da Yarn Store	92

Preface

I grew up in Voe in the fifties and sixties. My parents were both Adie's employees; so were many of the folk I knew. I spent school holidays working at Adie's, I finished jumpers for pocket money, I heard the stories and absorbed something of the lightsome, busy atmosphere that was still to be found there, and the busier times that people would always tell you about, and hark back to.

I didn't set out to write a detailed history of the Adie business, though such a book would be well worth writing. I just wanted to put something down on paper that might give a flavour of the kind of place that Adie's was, and a glimpse of at least some of the people who worked there. I am very much aware how disappointed some people will be at the amount of names and incidents I have not been able to include and to them I must apologise in advance.

This book has been a most interesting and enjoyable project. In particular, I have spent one of the most lightsome summers of my life in 2001, visiting, listening, asking questions and looking at photos! To everybody who has helped so willingly, and given me information, photographs, or advice, not to mention generous hospitality, I would like to express my grateful thanks.

Acknowledgments

Thanks must go to: The late Magnie Manson, Peter Hughson, Jamie Tulloch of South Voxter, and Jessie Couper.

Also to: James A. Adie, Anne Adie and Esme Findlay; Willie Hutchison, Jamie and Hazel Hutchison; Peggy Parkin and Joey Anderson; Marion Williamson; Maggie Brown, Kathleen Tait and Ian Tait; my parents-in-law Dodie and Mary Johnson; Andy and Babs Robertson; Annie Hall, Peggy Johnson and Jean Johnson; Chrissie Tait; Olive Gunn and Morag Hay; Andy Wood; Bertha and Thomas John Thompson, John and Helen Thompson; Bella and Maurice Hughson; Joyce Mackintosh, Drewie Johnson and Betty Sutherland; Tammie Robertson; Anna Johnson and Myra Thomason; Mimie Pearson; Ruby Johnson, Tina Johnson and Myra Irvine; Pete and Kathleen Blance; Anna Johnson, Bayview; Eileen Georgeson; Wilma Couper; Mabel Rendall; Leonard Cheyne; George P.S. Peterson; Frankie and Maggie Johnson; Charlie Laurenson; John Sutherland; Diane Wood. And thanks to Allan, for his encouragement.

Introduction

> At wan o'clock, da rodd wis black wi fock headin off for denner - as far as Hillcrest an da Hoga.
> *Annie Hall*

> I suppose it is a bit of an achievement tae a been sae lang, a whole 50 year, wi wan firm - especially when I only guid ta help oot for a fortnight.
> *Jamie Couper*

> What cam an guid dere, boys an lasses - fae aa ower.
> *Willie Hutchison*

The firm of T. M. Adie and Sons dominated life in Voe for well over a century. Thomas Adie sold his first groceries in 1830, when he was fifteen years of age, and thereafter he built up a family business which ran a farm and a general merchant's shop, and developed first into fishing and fish-curing and later into knitwear, bakery and tweed manufacture. The shop was only sold in 1991.

There were boom times and slumps; the fishing peaked in the 1870s, knitwear in the 1930s and tweed production in the 1950s. In good times, Adie's was a major employer whose importance to the north mainland of Shetland was considerable. Around 1950, for example, there were 95 on the payroll (though this also included some weavers working in Scalloway and others at home). There was an employees' dance about that time; Adie's workers, with partners, made for a busy hall floor.

The local community still remembers the firm's good record of trying to give employment wherever possible, at times when few opportunities existed elsewhere. Because of Adie's, few men in the area had to go to sea, local single women could find work, and married women had an outlet for their knitting. Staff valued good management and business sense, but what is most kindly recalled is this willingness to provide employment. This seems to have been a consistent element in the long history of the firm.

> Well, du sees, dem at wis evicted in Voe wisna just sae ill aff because dey wir *Voe*. An dey could get a bit of a job.........dryin fish, beach boys, carpenter wark, upkeep o boats, sail-makin...
> *W.H. referring to 19th century*

Efter da war I stoppit wirkin, dey wir dat mony men needin wark. Ted tried ta fin wark for dem whenever he could. Dey maistly aa got something, even if da wages wisna high.
Mary Leask/ Johnson, 1940s

Adie's gae a lot o employment. Something wis fun for schöl leavers ta do.
Myra Thomason, 1950s/60s

Adie's Buildings

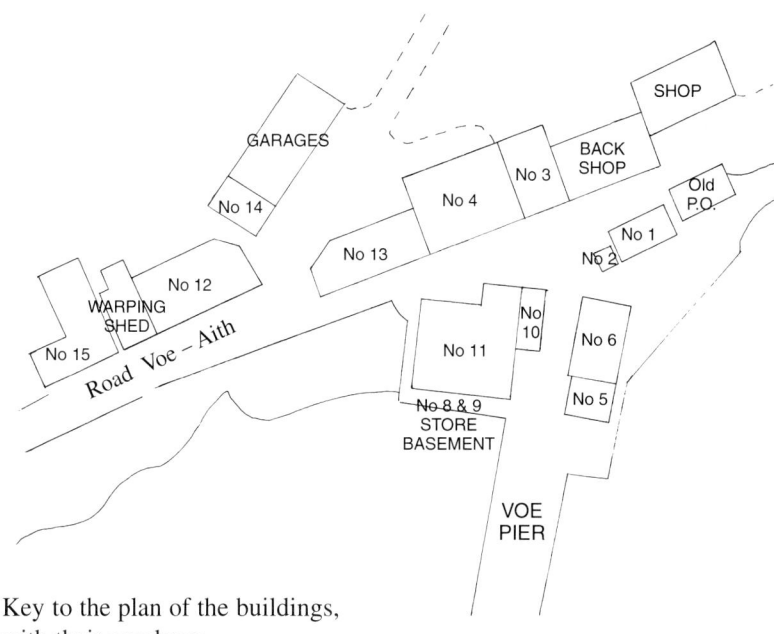

Key to the plan of the buildings,
with their numbers:

1. Meal store
2. Paraffin shed
3. Despatch room
4. Bakery
5. Scouring house
6. Drying loft
7. (under Number 6) Wool store
8.& 9. (both under Number 11) Store, used for salt in smack days
10. Coal shed
11. Knitwear, (in early days Sail Loft)
12. Weaving shed
13. Carpenter shed
14. Old scouring house, etc.
15. Picking shed

The warping shed did not have a number. When it became a warping shed, it was accessible from both the picking shed and the weaving shed. The garages, the old post office building and the shop itself did not have numbers either.

Special thanks to Pete Blance and Allan Johnson

Chapter 1
The Fishing Days

At a glance, any local person could find plenty of differences between this photograph and a modern view. It takes closer inspection to notice one important difference. The old photograph, taken in the very beginning of the 20th century, clearly shows the "drying beaches" of Voe.

Voe at the beginning of the 20th century. © **Shetland Museum**

Voe, of course, has no beaches to speak of, that is, no sand and precious little shingle. Neither does it naturally have big flat stones or anything suitable for the drying of fish in large quantities. The drying beaches were man-made, and extended well above the level of the present road, right to the wall of the garden of Bellevue. They were made by Adie's workers in the 19th century, in order to dry and cure fish for export.

T. M. Adie, whose father, Dr John Adie, had been involved in fish-curing, rented ling-curing stations in various places in Shetland, and tried herring-fishing, unsuccessfully at first. Real success came with the development of cod-fishing, and the firm sent smacks as far as Faroe, Rockall and Iceland. Business took off, and extended to Papa, Scalloway, Northmavine, Whalsay and Skerries. Voe itself was very busy by the late 1850s, and in the 1870s the firm became T.M. Adie and Sons.

From the Report into the Truck System, 1872:
> T. M. Adie employs about 400 fishermen. Has a factor and shop at Voe, Papa, Stenness and Skerries, employs 30 to 60 at curing. Has 5 vessels at Faeroe fishing Gave up hosiery in 1870. Employs beach boys Papa, Stenness, Skerries.

In the 1880s, Adie's again began herring-fishing, this time successfully. This was to outlast the cod-fishing, right into the early years of the 20th century, when, at last, sail-boats simply had to give way, being unable to compete with steam drifters.

Photo from the fishing days. © Shetland Museum

Fishing-smacks, in the cod-fishing days, varied in size. Some were ex-ocean-going yachts, bought cheap and converted, with sail plans made over. One was reputed to have been a former Revenue cutter and very fast, able to outsail the cutters of the day, who were in the business of checking returning Faroe smacks for contraband brandy and tobacco.

> Names of smacks owned by Adie's at one time or another: *Benita (or Benito), Experiment, Gypsy Queen, Granville, Hurricane, Lady Nightingale, Miranda, Noran, Petrel, Pioneer, Racer, Saucy Jack, Seamew, Star of the East, Stour, Walrus, William Barentz, John Kelly.*
> **James A. Adie**

Some of the smacks were "well-smacks". One section of the hold of a well-smack was water-tight, but had holes bored in, apparently at different angles, so that there was a constant through movement of sea water in this "well". Here prime cod could be kept alive and fresh, and so earn a bonus price when it was landed.

Landings of live fish were made at mainland ports, usually on the Humber. Sailing as far as this took up time which, in summer, a crew could not afford to lose. So live cod were only taken on the last trip of the season, which meant that the smack could carry on to e.g. Grimsby, before laying up for the winter.

The largest live catch ever landed by a Shetland boat was 1100 cod.

There were over a dozen men and boys in a fishing-smack crew. Fishing was done by hand-line, and each fisherman tallied up his own catch. The fish were usually split and wet-salted at sea. Trips lasted weeks or months.

Here is a description of the loading of a fishing smack, written by someone who himself sailed to the cod-fishing. We can imagine many scenes like this around the Voe pier:

> …salt based on the vessel's curing capacity - generally from thirty to forty tons - barrels for cod liver and for salting roes, tubs, draining vats - all the varied material needed for the fishing as well as food stores and water sufficient for from twelve to fifteen men for three months had to be shipped. Last and most important, the bait, usually mussels, were put in barrrels or bags, and kept alive in some sheltered sea-pond, ready for the day of sailing. Add to this several tons of coal, accommodation for the crew, spare sails, etc. and it can be imagined that those small vessels were loaded without reference to Plimsoll.
>
> Captain A. Halcrow, *The Sail Fishermen of Shetland*.

The early herring fishing, on the Atlantic side of Shetland, traditionally started in the first week of June, though the late (North Sea) fishing was the main one, from late July. Captain Halcrow lists the following vessels as Adie's boats, and describes them as "decked fishers": *Elizabeth, Lily, Mary Leslie, Ocean Queen, Viscount Arbuthnot*. These were not all based at Voe. It seems that there were two boats with the name Elizabeth. Other herring-boats owned or part-owned by Adie's included *Mary Ann, Welcome Home, Eclipse* and *Victoria*.

The *Viscount Arbuthnot* was broken up below Kurkigarth. The porch of the house of Kurkigarth and much of the croft fencing came from this boat.

Names of Smack Skippers

This is probably not a complete list and some of the initials may not be correct. There are no details of how long the man sailed for Adie's. Any date or other known details are given. If a boat name is mentioned, this does not mean that the man always skippered this particular boat.

Arthur Anderson		Hevdi, Grobsness
Magnus Anderson	1893	
J. Balfour		
Robert Balfour	1889	*Noran*
T. Balfour	1888	
J. Blance	1872	
Peter Blance	1897	*Seamew*
Robert Couper	1897	*Petrel*
Thomas Hall	1872	*Miranda*
Peter Hawick	1888	
? Hay	1879	
James Henderson		
John Hunter	1904	*Granville*
William Irvine, Delting	1871	married, age 33
John Jamieson, Voe	1880	*Pioneer*
J. Johnson		
James Johnson	1891	Scarvataing, Muckle Roe
John Laurenson, Delting	1871	married, age 53, *Saucy Jack*
W. Nicolson	1887	
Haldane Peterson	1871	single, age 40, *Lady Nightingale*
William Tait		

Crew of the *Gypsy Queen* in 1871
(Boat Census)

William Irvine	married	33	Master	Delting
John Sandison	unmarried	32	Mate	Northmavine
Thomas Couper	married	39	AB	Delting
Magnus Irvine	unmarried	27	AB	Delting
Charles Couper	married	28	AB	Delting
Wm. Williamson	unmarried	32	seaman	Northmavine
James Irvine	married	60	AB	Delting

James Williamson	unmarried	19	seaman	Lunnasting
Henry Hunter	married	29	AB	Nesting
William Hawick	unmarried	14	seaman/boy	Delting
Robert Johnstone	unmarried	17	seaman/boy	-
James Hawick	unmarried	17	seaman/boy	-
Gilbert Hunter	unmarried	16	seaman/boy	Nesting

Crew of the *Stour* in 1871

Christopher Dalziel	married	55	Mate	Aithsting
Andrew Coghill	married	42	AB	Delting
Wm. Georgeson	unmarried	21	seaman	Delting
John Leisk	unmarried	14	boy	Delting
John Georgeson	married	35	AB	Lunnasting
Magnus Anderson	unmarried	23	AB	Delting
Archibald Jacobson	married	57	AB	Delting
Thomas Lusk	married	32	seaman	Whalsay
Scott Rastor	married	48	AB	Northmavine
Hugh Sinclair	unmarried	24	seaman	Delting
Andrew Inkster	unmarried	28	seaman	Northmavine
Mitchell Georgeson	married	24	AB	Lunnasting
Thomas Nicolson	married	30	AB	Delting

Other crew names known:

From 1871:

Magnus Andrew	unmarried	19	seaman, *Benito*
John Greig	unmarried	18	boy, *Lady Nightingale*
John Abernethy	married	31	Northmavine, mate on *Saucy Jack*
Daniel Tulloch	unmarried	33	seaman, Northmavine, *Saucy Jack*
Charles Anderson	unmarried	35	seaman, Delting, *Saucy Jack*

From other dates:

William Anderson, Voe	1880 *Pioneer* (lost at Burra on her way from Leith where she had just been bought. Crew of three all saved.)
Robert Ramsay, Lerwick	1880 *Pioneer*
James (or John) Johnson, Kurkigarth, Voe	*Granville*
Robert Manson, Pund, Voe	*Granville*

The skipper's log

Part of the log of Adie's 66-ton smack *Seamew*, skippered by Peter Blance, was published in *The New Shetlander*, Voar, 1970. It dates from 1897, in the last years of the cod-fishing, and gives details of three trips, one to Faroe (eight weeks), one to Rockall and Faroe (nine and a half weeks) and one to Iceland (seven weeks). In between trips, the crew spent no more than a week at home, some of that time being taken up with discharging their catches, and preparing again for sea.

**From a drawing of a smack similar to the *Seamew*.
Courtesy of Pete Blance.**

First trip

They spent two days in March fitting out for the summer fishing, and sailed for Faroe on the 19th. The wind veered from North-north-east to East, they sailed N.W. x N., and they sighted land in Faroe at 3.00 pm on the 21st. Four more Shetland smacks were already on the grounds. As the *Seamew* moved around Faroe waters, plenty more smacks were to be seen; about 50 on the 1st of April, for example.

The weather was changeable and often rough. Catches varied; the smack *Granville*, by the 4th of April, had caught 1000 cod, while on Tuesday the 6th of April, Peter Blance spoke to "a Faroe smack who had been on the banks for two weeks and only caught 20 cod." To that date, the *Seamew's* biggest catch had been 290 cod, and she had lost a few days through bad weather. On Thursday the 8th of April, the skipper wrote "Have spoken several smacks and all report poor fishing." The next day, they caught 450 cod, and the following day, 430. Surely this was an improvement? Then of course, the next week brought more strong wind, sleet and snow.

On Sunday 18th April, they put into Klakwall to spend two days filling water tanks. Here they heard from the smacks *King Arthur* and *William Martin* that no fish were to be found at Rockall. For the remainder of their trip the fishing was patchy and the month of May brought even more strong gales:

Saturday, 8th; Wind hauled round to the N.W. and continued to blow gale force. Shipped a heavy sea and smashed our rails. All well on board.

On Thursday, 13th May, 1897, Peter Blance set sail for home at 1.00 pm, accompanied by the *Granville* and the *Walrus*. There were head winds for part of the next day, but they arrived in Voe at 4.00 pm on Saturday the 15th.

Total catch :4027 cod

Second trip

The *Seamew* set out for Rockall on Saturday, 22nd May, 1897, with the wind N.E. x E. They sighted Rona on Monday, 24th, fished a little between Rona and the Flannan Isles, and finally arrived in sight of Rockall at 10.00 am on Saturday, 29th May. Here they fished for two weeks, in mostly fine weather conditions, caught some cod, and a few tusk and saithe, but it didn't come to much. Only one other smack, the *Granville*, was with them.

Extracts from June log:

> Friday 11th: Fished until 4.30 p.m. Left for Faroe. The fishing at Rockall poor this summer.
>
> Saturday, 12th: Fresh S.S.W. wind. Logged 150 miles in 24 hours.
>
> Sunday, 13th: Wind S.S.W. moderate. Logged 104 miles for 24 hours.
>
> Monday, 14th: 11.00 p.m. Arrived off Maganess, Faroe. Spoke 'Granville'.

For the next five weeks, Peter Blance fished around Faroe, with generally better weather than on his previous trip. His best fishing day was Friday, 25th June, when the catch was up to 626 cod. Once July came in, catches dwindled. After the 371 caught on the 5th, the biggest catch on any one day was 47.

A disappointed crew set out for home on Wednesday, 21st July. With light winds and one day of calm, it took them till Sunday, 25th July to come in sight of Foula. On Monday, 26th July, after nine weeks at sea, only broken by two days ashore in Thorshavn, they lowered their lines on the Foula Bank for one last try before reaching home. They caught nothing.

> Tuesday, 27th, 6 p.m. Arrived and anchored at Voe. Crew went home till Friday.
>
> Friday, 30th: Worked all day discharging fish.
>
> Saturday, 31st: Worked all day discharging fish.

Total catch: 5108 cod, 157 tusk, 39 saithe.

NB. Changed days at Rockall! Not so many years earlier, in 1886, the shoals of cod were so dense that unbelievable-sounding stories were told about them, e.g. that they were found with one another's tails in their mouths. One of Adie's boats, the 38-ton *Benito*, had brought four full loads from Rockall to Voe in fifteen weeks.

Sailing speed: The *Stour*, (54 tons), an Adie's boat, seems to have held the speed record at this time. She once came 200 miles from Faroe to Voe in 17 hours.

Third trip

The *Seamew's* third trip that summer was to Iceland. As she was a well-smack, this would be the time for keeping a portion of her catch alive in the well.

It was not a particularly easy cargo. Heavy seas would create problems, and so would very calm weather, as the water in the well had to keep circulating. Putting into a port might kill the fish. Even when a well-smack finally arrived at her destination market, she would stay outside the harbour, tacking around until a fish broker's boat came to her.

The *Seamew* left Voe on Wednesday, 4th August, and took till Monday, 16th August to reach the fishing grounds. They sighted twelve other smacks fishing on the banks.

Once there, they soon learned that prospects were much better than anywhere else they had been that summer. The smack *Buttercup* reported already having caught 13,000 cod for their trip; the *William Martin* had caught 14,000. The *Seamew's* catches were much improved: 1016, 610,

1444, 1020, 800, 1174, 983 being some of the figures recorded over the next 5 weeks.

The trip had its moments. There were gales, and days of fog.

> Sunday 22nd: Spoke Walrus who has lost boat and broken her mainboom and is leaving for Shetland.
>
> Sunday 29th: Thick fog. Grounded on a shallow bank on the south side of Axer Fiord at 5.00 p.m. At 5.30 p.m. we run out a kedge and warp and pulled the smack afloat at 6.00 p.m. Sounded vessel around and found no apparent damage.
>
> Sunday 5th September: Fresh breeze from the south. We commenced tacking up Axer Fiord.
>
> Monday, 6th: Wind increased to moderate gale from the NNW. Had to put about and tack out of Axer Fiord.

By September, there were snow showers in Iceland. On Sunday, the 19th, they began their journey home.

> Sunday, 19th: 1.00 p.m. … left for Shetland. Strong NNW, set course to pass east of the Faroe Isles.
>
> Monday, 20th: Wind shifted in the morning to south dead ahead and continued dead ahead all day.
>
> Tuesday, 21st: Wind veered NW. 6.00 p.m. sighted Faroe on the starboard bow. 9.00 p.m. Svino abeam. Set course for Muckle Roe.
>
> Wednesday, 22nd: Wind light NW.
>
> Thursday, 23rd: Arrived at Voe. Crew discharged fish on Friday, 24th September.

Total catch: 12,337 cod. There is no indication of how much of this was live and would have been carried to a mainland market.

Note on the *Seamew*

The *Seamew* was built in Dundee in 1871 for T. M. Adie and Sons. She was said to be "the finest well-smack that ever came to Shetland" (Captain A.

Halcrow). A Blance man stood by at the building of her. This seems likely to have been Peter Blance's father, James Blance, as in 1871 Peter would have been five years old.

She was finally wrecked in 1903 in Hamar Voe. (No loss of life). The wreck site is marked on a map on display in Tangwick Haa museum, Shetland.

Peter Blance, smack skipper

Peter Blance, pictured here with his family, was born in 1866. He originally came from Calback, then lived in Muckle Roe, then the Haa of Grobsness, and finally Newhouse, Voe. His wife was Margaret Hall or Johnson, from Roe, and his children Lowrie, Maggie, Jamie and Peter Blance. Peter, the youngest, (father of Pete Blance, Houll, Voe) was born in Newhouse in 1899.

Peter Blance left Adie's and went to skipper a cargo smack. He intended to buy his own boat and do coastal trade. Sadly, he drowned in the harbour at Fortrose, the Black Isle, 14th November, 1907. He was a good swimmer, but fell between the boat and the pier. He was 41 years old. Strangely, his father, James Blance, had also drowned at the same age.

His son Peter, who was eight in 1907, remembered very little of his seaman father, as he was so often away.

His daughter Maggie was the mother of Peter Anderson of Flett, and Joey Anderson and Peggy Parkin of Newhouse.

From left to right: back) **Maggie of Flett (a neighbour), Lowrie, Peter Blance, Maggie, Margaret, holding young Peter, (front) Jamie Blance.**

A smuggling yarn

From a tape-recording of Willie Hutchison, Hillend, Voe:

Da smacks wid come in, an dey hed dis geos whaar dey wid hoid dis braandy an tobaacha fae Faroe. Dey wid try an come in ida darkenin, aff o da coast o Shetland, an dey wid be closin laand in Shetland wi da dark. An dan dey pat der braandy an tobaacha ashore, an dey sailed inta Voe.

Weel, Adie's, dey said, never seemed dem. Dey didn't want ta interfere or know anything aboot dat. But, you see, da Revenue cutter wanted ta know all aboot dat! He wis sometimes patrollin oot aroond da coast. An du might a been lucky ever sae aft, an maybe never fell in wi him, but sometime, somehow, he maybe catched up wi dee, an dan it wis too bad!

Dey wir none at I ever heard o bein catched, but dey wir wan time, aff o da back o Papa, at dey saw her comin, da Revenue ship. An da skipper o da smack wis Peter Blance, fae Newhouse. Dey said he wis a good seaman, an knew his coast properly.

"Da only wye" he says, " at we're goin ta get clear o dem is, we'll hae ta close Papa wi dem." Dey wid hae ta go aroond some stack. An when she guid aroond dat stack, dey said, she just could glide trow. Dan he set her awey towards Aid.

Dey got up aroond da back o Papa Little, an dan ... da cutter sailed right on for Voe, for he wid catch dem in at Voe. An dey took da sails aff o her, an just hed her hove-to aff o Queenster. Dey pat two men wi a boat ashore wi all dis contraband, an dey hoidit it atil a roog somewye up aboot Queenster. Dey left dat boat an da two men an dey sailed on inta Voe.

When dey cam inta Voe, dan he wis lyin at da pier, da Customs man, an dey reckoned at he wis damnable peeved! He said dey'd gotten him dis time, but wan ta h--- o dem wid get him again!

Adie cam doon an hed nothing ta say, but he lookit, an he missed dis two men. So he hed a fly chance, an he said, "Are you aa right?" An dis old fellow said, oh yea, yea, dey wir ower weel! He kent dan, but dat wis all da questions asked.

An dis two men cam rowin in awey sometime troo da night wi da boat, an dan dey guid an shared oot da braandy an da tobaacha! Da maist o dat journeys wis taen trow da hill, never near da coast ava.

NB. The Adies were not above benefiting a little from their crews' smuggling activities. There was a known hiding-place in Voe House where contraband could be kept out of sight of visiting officialdom.

Shoreside Stories

The sail-loft is on the far right; only part of it can be seen here.   © Shetland Museum

Fishing, fish-curing and boat maintenance provided plenty of employment. Willie Hutchison, grandfather of the present Willie of Hillend, went to work as a carpenter in the Voe sail-loft, from about the age of thirteen or fourteen. This would have been about 1870, at the height of the fishing boom.

Willie described himself as "second generation oot o Whalsa"; his father, John Hutchison, was originally a Whalsay man. Willie spent most of his working life at Adie's,

Willie Hutchison.   Courtesy of Hutchison, Hillend.

weathering some periods of slack time when things were not so busy. At one time he serviced boats to Leslie of Laxfirth, then work picked up again in Voe. His last job in Voe was working the carding-machine.

Willie's home was Hillside, above the Tagon junction. He died in April 1947, in his 90th year, and is fondly remembered. Hillside is now occupied by Leonard and Barbara Cheyne; Leonard is Willie's great-grandson.

Boats needed repair and constant upkeep. Sails had to be cut, then rope-mountings, ropes, blocks, etc. were needed from the stocks kept in store. The sail-loft was peopled with "characters", old ex-deep-sea sailing men, such as Arthur Moar, of Aith. He was a former Royal Navy man, and an expert sail-cutter. Another man had a notorious drink problem. He would work for a few weeks, then have a binge and get the sack. Then he would go to work to Pole's in Mossbank, and a few weeks later the pattern would repeat itself and he'd be back again at Adie's. He was such a good hand that it was considered worthwhile to have him, even for a few weeks at a time!

An English schooner once anchored in the voe, and as it had a torn sail, the skipper asked Adie's to send him a man to do a repair job. The man never returned and the story circulated that he must have slipped over the side of the ship, an accident possibly caused by too much of the skipper's brandy. A day or so later, his body washed ashore below Voe House and was found in the early morning as work was starting at Adie's.

A young local man ("a wild, daft fellow") seized the woollen cap from the head of the dead man, put it on his own head, and went dancing into the shop. The shop was a low stone building, none too well-lit, and the cap was a familiar one. The elderly shop foreman, it is said, nearly fainted with shock.

This story has a postscript: The young practical joker later went to Australia. Some years afterwards, a local sailing man was on a ship which put in at a small Australian port. A gold wagon in the area had been attacked by "bushrangers", there had been a gun-battle, and some of the bushrangers had been shot dead. Their bodies were lying on a wooden jetty, covered with a tarpaulin.

For some unknown reason, the Shetland sailor lifted a corner of the tarpaulin. To his amazement, he recognised one of the dead faces. He had no doubt of it, he said, he was quite sure. It was the same boy, the "wild, daft fellow" who had taken the dead man's cap that strange morning in Voe. He had ended his days as a bandit.

Diphtheria

In May 1891, *The Shetland News* reported that the smack *Walrus* had arrived at Voe with four diphtheria cases on board. The men were taken ashore and Dr Yule summoned from Lerwick.

> "...proper remedies were applied, and the men are now going on well. Every precaution was taken in the way of disinfecting the skipper and crew."

Ice Damage

The 40-ton *Alarm*, 52 years old but only owned by Adie's for a year, sank at anchor at Voe on 17th February, 1895, while carrying coal. She was sunk by ice in the voe.

There is a model of the *Alarm* in Shetland Museum.

The *Venus*

Another wreck, this big 191-ton ship became a loss in 1895. Adie's then bought her, moored her in the voe and used her as a coal hulk. Later, she was beached at the NW side of the pier, as can be seen in early photos. A door was cut in her side and she was used as a store. Later still, she was broken up, but pieces of her keel timbers could still be seen with a spring ebb tide as late as 1990.

A peerie story from shoreside Thorshavn

From the log of the *Granville*, 1897:

> 7th July: Came to anchor in Thorshaven at 5 o'clock and reported. Boat went in to get water, came back, two hands ashore got themselves into some trouble, and were shut up for the night.
>
> 8th July: The two hands came back at half-past ten forenoon.

Chapter 2
The Shops, the Slump and the First World War

T. M. Adie had set up shop in 1830 in a small way, at the age of fifteen, selling goods from home in the Old House of Voe, roughly where Burnside stands now. "Voe" was a croft name which, thanks to "Adie's of Voe" eventuually came to be applied to the whole village, completely eclipsing the old name "Olnafirth".

Old house of Voe on left. This house was completely demolished. Brungasta on right, built 1903. Hoga in background. © Shetland Museum

As business grew, a shop was built near the pier. A busy general merchant's shop at the heart of a thriving fishing business needs quite a few staff. Later on, in the early years of the new century, around 1910, a

Shop staff. Date and identities uncertain. Perhaps the bearded man is Gilbert Hay and one of the tall lasses Osla Hay.
© Shetland Museum

15

second, larger shop was built, with stone from the newly-opened Voe quarry. This was to be Adie's shop as people today remember it, a high-ceilinged main shop with an upper floor and an office section, and linked to the old shop building, which would now become known as the back shop. So it would be for almost the whole of the 20th century

The house of Brungasta was built in 1903. It consisted of two semi-detached halves, and one side of Brungasta became home to Gilbert Hay, who for many years was shop manager. He died in 1924, aged 85, and is still remembered in Voe. ("A big man laek all da Hays" - W.H.) His wife was Ann Anderson from the Hoga, Voe, and they had seven of a family.

Their oldest daughter, Osla, later became, in her turn, shop manager, and then boss of the hosiery workers. Babsy died in 1905, at the age of eighteen. Maggie, the youngest daughter, became Mrs McPherson and lived in Liverpool. Two of the four sons emigrated. The boy in the picture may be Bertie, youngest of the family, who went out to Hawaii, or Bobby, who went to New Zealand.

Gilbert Hay and some of his family. © Shetland Museum

When the fishing faded, there was a slack period at Voe for a while. The farm and the shop continued, with knitted goods being bought in, or rather, exchanged for groceries, as was the system then. A new venture was tried in 1910, when a carding-machine was installed in a shed where the weaving shed was later to stand. It was a big, complex machine, driven by a steam engine, and was still in operation in the 1920s, but it was not a great asset and was later dismantled.

The outbreak of the First World War, however, brought new developments.

James Adie, grandson of T. M., was a Lieutenant in the RNVR, and an artillery gun-crew under his command became based in Voe. This was part of the shore preparation to counter submarine attacks, which were so much feared in the war years. Charts have been found with lines of fire plotted from the Point of Mulla. The gun was housed in a shed built for the purpose at Adie's. Next to it, another wooden building was erected as gun crew accommodation. There were three navy men and four or five local men in the gun crew, and John Wood, later a well-known Adie's van driver, was petty officer in charge at one stage.

The gun shed can still be seen, at the end of the old weaving shed, (now a joinery workshop). On the other side of the gun shed there is now a private house, but part of this house was originally the gun-crew accommodation, and was first known as the "Raven's Rest". Whether this was an official address or a local nickname, the name was used for years after the First World War.

Magnie Manson was a young bairn at the Pund in the First World War. From his home, he watched the comings and goings of boats in the voe. Not fishing-boats, though. Folk said they used to be fishing-boats, but now they were busy running to the supply ship *Gibraltar* out in Busta Voe. Sometimes, sailors would appear at the croft door, asking if there were any eggs to be had, or chickens to buy.

Magnie Manson and his mother Teena.
© **Ramsay, photo courtesy of Bella Hughson.**

Swarbacks Minn, Busta Voe and Olnafirth had become home to the Royal Navy 10th Cruiser Squadron. It needed steady supplies of all kinds. It was noticeable that the slaughter-house next to Adie's stables was now in frequent use. Leslie of Laxfirth was said to be coming there to slaughter kye.

Betty Moffat from Aith, (mother of Chrissie Tait, Ashbank, East Burrafirth), was a shop assistant during the war years. She remembered how, "if nae man body wis aroond", she would help Osla Hay to cut up the meat for delivery to the Navy. Osla was a tall, strong woman, and could do this job as well as a man.

The Squadron also needed fresh bread, in large quantities. The big ships must have had their own bakers on board; if any of them were anchored near enough, with an on-lying wind, the folk at the croft of Kurkigarth used to be able to smell the newly-baked bread. However, there were so many smaller vessels and support craft that obviously more bread was needed than the Navy itself could supply.

Fresh bread could sometimes be obtained at Voe. As far back as 1881, for example, T. M. Adie wrote to the Scalloway bakery, requesting that fresh bread be sent to Voe with the fortnightly steamer. But now, here was a demand that might be met. All you needed was premises, equipment, and a trained baker or two.

Inside the old bakery oven, before it was demolished.

There was a sizeable building, next to the old shop, which had once held paint and other boat stores, but now lay idle. A bakery oven was built in here, and the Voe bakery began. With a ready-made market on its doorstep, it got off to a promising start.

The oven was built by a man called Denham. Building a brick oven is very specialised work. Many years later, in the 1990s, that first oven was finally removed – it was a major demolition job – and replaced by an electric oven. Again the installation was done by a specialist firm from south. The firm was run by a man called Andrew Denham. He was either a grandson or a grand nephew of the man who built the first oven.

A major demolition job!

Chapter 3
The Twenties and Thirties

Building up: the 1920s

It got busier in Voe efter I cam. (1925)   *Jessie Nicolson/ Couper*

To name but a few of the folk that were dere when I cam, in 1925: Annabel (Cheyne)'s great-grandfather, Willie Hutchison, Myra (Thomason)'s grandfather, Willie Brown, Baabie Balfour, Osla Hay, Lowrie Umphray, and many more....

Jamie Couper, retiring in 1975

By 1925, Adie's was on the up. Edward (Ted) Adie had taken over the business in 1922, in partnership with his eldest sister, Myra I. C. Adie (always known as Miss Adie). Gradually the business began to grow and thrive again.

The bakery continued. A lot of south men came up to work as bakers, some staying longer than others. Some names have been remembered: Marshall, a foreman baker in the 20s, Willie Geddes, another foreman baker, and Willie Hughes, from the Edinburgh area, who married a Voe lass, Mary Johnson of Sursetter. There was also Gilbert Hunter from Nesting, uncle to Benjie Hunter. He was a baker at Voe in the early 20s, before going on to become part of the Lerwick bakery firm of Hunter, Irvine and Tait.

Two young Voe men, Lowrie Brown, Kirkhouse, and Johnny Johnson, Hillend, became bakers in the 20s. They were joined by Robbie Jamieson, who originally came from Unst. Robbie was an experienced baker who had worked in Edinburgh and Sandwick.

Voe bakers, early 20s. Back left, Benjie Johnson, Sursetter, who may have been the driver, others unknown. Front row; left to right: Lowrie Brown, unknown, Willie Hughes, Gilbert Hunter. Photo courtesy of Frankie Johnson

Voe bakers, probably about 1930. Left to right: Johnny Johnson, Willie Hughes, Robbie Jamieson, Willie Geddes.

The bakery also needed despatch room staff, who packed biscuits etc., made up orders and loaded vans. This is where Jamie Couper of Hamars came, in 1925, "to help oot for a fortnight."

The bakery had begun as early as 1920 to send out deliveries. By and by, two vanloads of loaf and biscuits were being sent every week to Lerwick, helping to supply all the peerie shops that had sprung up around the town in the high days of the herring fishing. Regular deliveries were made to shops in other districts, Northmavine, Walls, Sandness and Scalloway.

One of Magnie Anderson's first duties at Voe was to accompany a van driver on the Northmavine run. Perhaps early vans were a bit on the light side? Apparently, the fully loaded van could not make it up the steep slope of the Virdins on the north side of Mavis Grind! So half the cargo was unloaded at the foot of the brae, the other half at the top, then the van returned to the foot to re-load the first half and so on!

John Wood, van driver.

One of Adie's best-known drivers was John Wood, originally from Scarvataing, Muckle Roe (see opposite).

John probably started driving for Adie's in the very early 1920s, after previously working at the Olna whaling station. In 1921, John had married Annie Anderson, from the Hoga, Voe, and come to live at the Hoga. By the time their second son was born in 1924, the family was living in accommodation provided by the firm, one of the three "widden hooses" built next to Brungasta.

Voe about 1930. Three widden hooses in a row on right of picture. Large house next to them is Brungasta. Voe House, (built about 1862), almost in centre of picture, Bellevue, (built about 1870), a little further along. Tall house gable on in distance is the old manse. On the far hillside are Upper and Lower Hillend, above and below the high road. White house in foreground is the Pund. © Shetland Museum

The widden hooses were buildings from former fishing stations, brought to Voe and adapted. Over four decades they housed dozens of Adie's workers, some staying for a short time and others for years. At one time, there were actually *three* workers by the name of John Wood living there! Couples and single people were normally allocated one room, with some families getting two. It was crowded and there was little privacy, but it was a rent-free roof over your head, and handy with the job, and nobody in those days was used to having the luxury of much individual space.

This photo shows another long-term worker at Voe, Magnie Couper, often known as Peerie Magnie. He was certainly working on the farm from at least 1925 and he was its mainstay until well after the war when he retired. He was married to Ellie Hughson of Holligarth, Collafirth, and they, too, lived in the widden hooses, with their children Andy (seen here) and Mootie.

With the house of Brungasta also available for staff accommodation, Adie's was in a position to employ key workers from other areas than Voe. The nearby old manse, (site of the present-day "Fagradal") was also part of the firm's housing stock. All the firm's accommodation was rent-free.

Magnie Couper and son.
Courtesy of Delting History Group.

"Whan did aa da trees come?"

Nowadays, the trees are so much a part of Voe that in old photos the place looks a bit strange without them. They were probably not all planted at the same time, but many of the garden trees date from about or slightly before 1930. There was a man from south in charge of the planting, and young Jamie Johnson of the Hillend, brother to Dodie Johnson, worked with him to plant the trees. It was Jamie's first job at Voe, and he continued to work in the garden, and especially on the farm, until he and his family left Shetland in the early 1950s.

The *Ivy*, multi-purpose vessel

Flour for the bakery, together with other shop supplies, was brought in by the "Westside" steamer, which came from Leith via Aberdeen, Stromness and Scalloway, and called at Voe once a fortnight from the 1880s until about the end of the 1920s.

The steamer could never put in at the Voe pier; there was always a flit-boat of some kind, for example, the old *Ivy*, quite a sizeable boat, with sails and a 26 h.p. Kelvin engine. She was a former herring-boat, and had had the reputation of being a lucky boat. She was used for other purposes than meeting the steamer, e.g. transporting animals. The *Ivy* is well-remembered, even by people who never saw her, as she was immortalised in humorous verse by Magnie Anderson, after one stormy trip to Papa Stour.

Magnie in later life, was always known as Magnie o da Hoga, but he came from Kirkhouse, and was still living there at the time of the poem.

The voyage was fraught with problems: sails, ropes, the bogie stove and the captain's back, not to mention the weather! The poem has 58 verses in all. Here are some of them.

Magnie Anderson. © Abernethy
Photo courtesy of Tina Johnson.

The *Ivy* in the Cattle Trade

A rhyme I'll have to make myself,
Since none of you will try,
About the little barque that went out west
To bring in the Papa kye.

It was the 16th of October
In 1925
When the Ivy sailed for Papa Stour,
Her crew and captain five.

. . . The last time she had been at sea
Her mainsail tore in rags,
But Jimmie Johnson had patched it up   (Newhouse)
With Demerara sugar bags.

. . . Jerry, he was carpenter,   (Hutchison, Newhouse)
And Broonie, he was mate.   (Willie, Kirkhouse)
Our engineer was Jamieson,   (Peter, widden hooses)
Mechanic up to date.

Our captain's name was old Bob Coutts,   (Evrigarth, Papa,
At the wheel he there stood fast   now widden hooses)
And one lonely Kirkhouse sailor   (Magnie himself)
Signed on before the mast.

(It took time and trouble to get to Papa, and once there . . .)

We could not swim the cattle off
It was such a heavy swell
So it was declared a hopeless case
And it freshened in the gale.

Then they all took their cattle
And went merrily for home
And left the mariners of Voe
To toil upon the foam.

Our captain purchased tatties
To supply his noble crew
And we went to Geordie Fraser's   (East Biggins, grandfather of
And got reestit piltocks too.   G.P.S. Peterson)

. . . Then we gave her every link of chain
As she did reel and dance
And now the crew must stick with her
And let her take her chance.

. . . As the daylight, it came in,
The wind, it went, at length,
Creeping round in our favour
Decreasing in its strength.

. . . We soon had fourteen cattle aboard
And some were for the sale,
The remainder and four ponies
Belonging to R.L.   (a buyer)

. . . A heavy swell was in the firth
But favoured by the wind were we.
An hour and forty minutes
Took us past Vementry.

. . . When at last we made our appearance
For help we did not lack,

None so glad as Mr. Adie
To see us safely back.

Then our noble boss abraided us
With whisky in galore,
A straight man, and kind-hearted,
And what is wanted more?

So our adventures were forgot,
Johnny Walker made us nod,
For we were all half-seas across
As we went up the rodd!

Note on house names: several houses go by the name of Newhouse, and more than one was known as Kirkhouse.

The Papa Kye: kye often came from Papa to be sold in Voe. They used to be turned into the Mill Park until the sale took place.

A Sandwick lass comes north

Young Jessie Nicolson waited anxiously at the Market Cross in Lerwick. It was 1925, and she was on her way north to Voe to take up a job as a shop assistant at Adie's. A van was supposed to have picked her up ages ago, but there was still no sign of any van. What should she do?

A phone call in 1925 was less easily made than nowadays, but she found a phone and rang Voe. Mr Adie told her to hire a car from John Leask's and he would foot the bill.

So an hour or so later, she was nearing Voe, in rather posher transport than she had expected. She had never in her

Jessie Nicolson (Couper), Shop Assistant, 1925-1940.

life been north of Lerwick before, and always remembered her first journey down the steep Loch Brae to Adie's:

"We seemed ta geng doon, an doon, an doon! I windered just whaar we were goin!"

And so Jessie arrived at the shop where she would work for fifteen years, and the village where she would spend the rest of her life.

For six weeks, she stayed in the old manse, but then moved to a room in Brungasta, as the manse was about to be renovated.

Shop staff in 1925:

> Osla Hay, manager, about to leave
> Peter Johnson, Sursetter, who would become shop manager and hold that job till he retired
> Peter Johnson, Hillside
> Jamie Anderson, Hoga
> And Jessie, newly-arrived

The clerkess in the office around this time, or soon after, was Lizzie Inkster, from Burra. She was later to marry Jamie Anderson from the shop.

Things were changing in Voe in 1925. The carding-machine was still in operation, but not for much longer. Two other workers moved with Jessie from the old manse to Brungasta. One was Tom Robson, a Borders weaver brought to Shetland by Adie's, the first weaver on the premises in Voe. The other was Willa Tulloch, Kurkigarth, who was employed to put Adie's trademark on hosiery.

Knitwear – a changing scene

The hosiery system was about to change dramatically, but in 1925, all knitting was done by hand. Some was done on the premises, but far more was done at home and brought to Adie's so that it could be exchanged for groceries and other needful items from the shop.

Generations of Shetland lasses were brought up to know the importance of never being "haand idle". Only in recent, more prosperous times has that principle been allowed to lapse. Perhaps we have forgotten just how important hand-knitting used to be. In the 1920s, when Jessie came down from Brungasta to start work in the shop in the morning, there was often a queue of people waiting for the place to open. They came from a wide area, too.

From *The Shetland News*, 28th September, 1922:

> ## THOMAS M. ADIE & SONS,
> ## VOE.
>
> We have an unprecedented demand for all kinds of Shetland Hosiery this season, and are in immediate requirement of the following articles:—
>
> 12,000 WHITE SPENCERS.
> 1,700 WHITE SHAWLS.
> 1,800 GREY SHAWLS.
> 2,800 GREY SHAWLS, with Shaded Borders.
> 4,000 MOORAT, FAWN, and GREY JUMPERS, with Fair Isle Borders; Colours and Patterns must be good
> A number of MOORAT, FAWN, and GREY SCARFS, with Fair Isle Borders.
> 250 WHITE JUMPERS, with Fair Isle Borders.
> 4,000 MOORAT, FAWN, and GREY JUMPERS, with Openwork Insertion at foot, no Neck, and Sleeves.
> 250 WHITE JUMPERS, with Openwork Insertion.
> 300 MOORAT and GREY Fine Lace SKIRTS, with JUMPERS to match.
> 300 MOORAT, GREY, and FAWN Fine Lace JUMPERS, with 'V Neck and Long Sleeves.
> Fine WHITE CAMISOLES, SPENCERS, VESTS, PRINCESS PETTICOATS, Etc. All in the Fine Unst Yarn.
>
> We solicit all knitters who are unable to bring us their hosiery to send it by post, when prompt attention will be given to all parcels received.
> All parcels should have return postage enclosed.

The system was this:

(1) Take your hap, spencer, gloves or whatever you had to Miss Adie and see if she would buy it.

(2) If she said it was acceptable, go to Willa Tulloch and have the trademark sewn on.

(3) Go back to Miss Adie and get a "line" with the value of the hosiery written on it.

(4) Then exchange your line for goods at the shop. You could have cash, but usually people opted for goods.

It used to be said that taking your hosiery to Voe was a day's work – going there, going through the procedure, and getting home again!

Stories are sometimes told of women sitting up all night to get spencers ready for the morning or scorching a hap at the fire in a vain attempt to hurry it dry. The stories are true. Times were often hard; knitting was currency, and continued to be so for many years to come.

Baabie Balfour of Hubansetter, (on right of picture) and Dolly Brown of Kirkhouse, Voe.

Adie's had merchant customers in the south who bought the hand-knits. In 1927, some staff went to take part in an exhibition in London. Baabie Balfour of Hubansetter, (on right of picture) and Dolly Brown of Kirkhouse, Voe, are here seen demonstrating spinning and hand-knitting to a no doubt curious audience. Tom Robson is probably on the "loom at work" mentioned in the poster behind them.

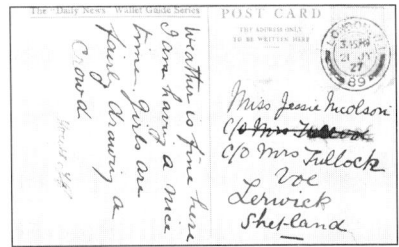

Postcard to Jessie from London exhibition.

Adie's would continue to buy in and sell on hand-knits, but in the late 1920s, just as the weaving was beginning to develop, the firm began another new venture. The first knitting machines were brought in, and an instructress from Liverpool came to Voe to train the first machinist. This was Dolly Brown.

Dolly, who was born in 1902, had already been working at Voe for some time, doing a variety of jobs. She had been a servant in Voe House, which was often busy with visitors and paying guests. She had washed hosiery, with Baabie Balfour, and worked at the carding-machine with Maggie Sutherland (later Grains), of the Old Schoolhouse, Voe.

The new knitting machine was called a HARRISON, and Dolly was trained to use it in a week or so. Then she, in her turn, trained Maggie

Dolly Brown (Thomason).
Photo courtesy of Myra Thomason

Maggie Sutherland (Grains).

Sutherland. The two pioneers worked in the old post office building, across the road from the shop. To begin with, they were meant to keep quiet about what they were doing. If any tourist or visitor came along they threw a cloth over the new-fangled machine!

Soon, the old sail-loft would be adapted to house a growing number of knitting-machines and young machinists, each new lass who arrived being trained by an old hand. They would be supported by back-up staff of finishers and examiners. Nobody called the place the sail-loft any more, except older people like Willie Hutchison of Hillside, who had spent too much of his working life in it to call it anything else. Now, and for most of the century, it would be known as "Number Eleven".

Dolly Brown left Voe to get married and became Dolly Thomason, in March, 1930.

The First Weavers

Just as hand-knitting had been bought in by Adie's, so too had home-woven tweed. (There had been a market for tweed at various times over many years; in the nineteenth century, T. M. had even ordered in tweed from Stonehaven.) When the firm began to weave tweed on the premises, the first local weaver to be trained was young Willie Hutchison, (now of the Hillend).

Right: Tom Robson.
Photo courtesy of Bertha Thompson.

Left: Willie Hutchison.
Photo courtesy of Willie Hutchison.

Willie came to Adie's in February, 1927. It was his first job. He was trained by Tom Robson from the Borders. There was a second weaver from south, John Dawson. Willie liked both men and found them fine to work with. There were three hand-looms in the former "Raven's Rest" where the First World War gun crew used to stay. The weavers at that time did their own warping.

Tom Robson was from Haddington. He was a former First World War soldier, and carried a bullet scar along his right jaw. Although he and his two brothers had returned safely from the war, his uncle's boys, all five of them, died. Remembrance Day every year was a difficult time for him. He moved from Voe to Scalloway, still employed by Adie's, and then went to Orkney to work for Gardiner's.

Why was it necessary to bring up weavers from south, if there had been hand-looms in croft-houses for many a year? The answer is changing technology. The new handlooms were spring-looms, which were different and much faster.

Manufacturing tweed is not just about using a loom. Firstly, the warp (length-wise) threads must be set up in the correct sequence and length for the loom. This is *warping*, a very important and quite complex job. The more complicated the loom and the pattern, the more painstaking is the warping process.

The yarn, which comes in bulk, must be wound onto reels of a suitable size for the weaver to use. Later, there would be a machine for "*windin pirms*" – but, when this is done by hand, it's a simple but monotonous job if ever there was one! Aching arm muscles, the smell of greasy tweed yarn in a sunless room – no wonder the Vidlin lass said, when asked by Miss Adie why she was standing at the outside door, "I'm just haein a breath o air. A galley slave gets nae less!"

View of Voe taken before mid-thirties. On left is the picking shed, probably still in its "Raven's Rest" form. The dark building to its right is the carding-shed, with the old gun-shed in between. This was used as a garage. Behind the carding-shed is Number Fourteen. A road goes up past Fourteen to the stables, left, and Voe House, right. Next in line along from the carding-shed is the Carpenters' shed, then the bakery. The building on the pier is old Number Seven. On the way up the brae, the widden hooses can be seen behind the house of Brungasta. On the hillside is first Kirkhouse, (this particular house also known as the Green Knowe at one time), then some of the houses of Newhouse, with Flett the topmost house.

© Shetland Museum

After the length ("wub") of tweed was woven, it was usually checked twice, once while still greasy from the loom, when knots and any minor weaving errors would be sorted out. This was *greasy-mending*. The tweed would then be washed and dried. After that it was checked again (*clean-mending*). This involved trimming off loose ends of thread, and picking off with tweezers any naps or other imperfections in the yarn. The checking process was also known as "*pickin tweed*" and the place it was always done, the old "Raven's Rest" where the first looms stood, became known as the "Picking Shed". It is still known by this name today, although it is now a private house.

The second local weaver to be trained was Peter Jamieson, later of Klonisburn, who at that time was living in the widden hooses; his brother John would join later. Their father, Robbie, worked in the bakery. (The Jamieson family came from Unst.)

Peter Jamieson standing on right.
Photo courtesy of Mabel Rendall.

In 1928, Magnie Manson of Pund, now seventeen years old, started work. His first job was picking tweed. This he did for a year or so. It became normal practice to start tweed work by either picking tweed, scouring tweed or windin pirms – or a mixture of the three. By and by, boys might get the chance to graduate to weaving. (There were no women weavers at this time; it was seen as a man's job.) Magnie Manson would be trained to weave by Willie Hutchison; both Robson and Dawson would then have left Voe. They left the weaving well established, with more looms under way, some in the old carding-shed.

Tweed and hosiery yarn was all bought in from south spinning mills eventually, but up to the early thirties at least, yarn was still being homespun. The wool arrived at the spinner's house in a big squat coil of carded "rowers", called a "knock". This was a precise quantity, so many rowers per knock. (The carding would also have been done south, though presumably not in the days of the carding-machine). If it was to be tweed yarn, apparently, it was spun and left as single-ply, whereas hosiery yarn would be twined.

Another of the first weavers was Magnie Anderson, Kirkhouse (later of Hoga). He was trained by John Dawson, and was already weaving tweed at the time of his marriage in 1929.

Upstairs, Downstairs in Voe House

In January, 1929, Magnie Anderson married Betty Wood, from Muckle Roe, who was cook at Voe House. Voe House and Bellevue were Adie family homes and both employed domestic staff.

Betty had started work on 27th April, 1927, a date which stuck in everyone's memory as a terrible day of blizzard. Every man was out seeking lambs and looking to animals.

Betty, shown here dressed suitably to wait at the evening dining-table, had previously been employed in Busta House, and liked domestic service, though the hours were long and the work often very tiring. Voe House was no exception, with family, visitors and guests to cater for. There was one guest who would never be forgotten by Betty, when at the end of her usual long stint in the evening, he gave her his dog to wash! Unable to refuse or complain, she duly scrubbed the animal, then later felt a bit guilty: "Guid forgie me, I scrubbit his paws till he yalkit!"

As part of her work, Betty churned butter and made not only kirnmylk but also cheese, using rennet obtained from Edinburgh. She continued to do this even after she married and went to live at the Hoga.

Betty Wood (Anderson).
Photo courtesy of Tina Johnson.

Life seems to have been quite formal in Voe House. If there was a letter to deliver to any of the family, for example, you had to fetch a silver tray to place it on – even if you met the person first! The servants in the dining-room were completely ignored and simply expected not to repeat what was said in front of them.

Meanwhile, backstage in the kitchen, there were the usual hushed-up crises, for example:

Dolly Brown and Betty Wood

Dolly: Oh Betty, Betty, da tail is come aff!
Betty: Come aff? Lat me see!
Dolly: Oh isn' dat awful, an she said at da troot hed ta be served whole apo da plate! Oh, what'll we dö???
Betty: (decisively, acting as she speaks) Stick da tail back on an never say a wird! Dey canna aet him whole!

Helen Jamieson, East Dyke, Lower Skelberry, and Mary Jamieson, Tarrarit (later Clark)

Mary: So is it yon man ida plus-fowers at's sae fussy?
Helen: Yes, he winna aet white eggs, he'll only hae broon.
Mary: Broon eggs? But we're not hed a broon egg here in monts.
Helen: Weel, what can we dö, tinks du?
Mary: I'll tell dee what. We'll boil da white eens in tay!

Mobile Shop

Towards the end of the 20s the first "shop van" was sent out, laden with groceries to sell. All the common bulk supplies, such as meal and flour, were made up in half-stone bags for the van.

Jamie Anderson, Hoga, one of the shop assistants, agreed to drive the van, and do the selling. Later, it would become common practice to send both a driver and a shop assistant. Shop vans soon became an important part of everyday life.

Soap, Soda and Sulphur

From the days of hand-knitting and home-woven tweed, there had been a need for washing facilities at Adie's, especially for hosiery, though Katy Blance, sister of the smack skipper Peter Blance, used to speak about washing tweed at Voe.

Washing was done in Number 14 for many years, a high wooden shed always referred to simply as "Fourteen". There was a big stove with a water tank (fed from a tank in the garden of Bellevue), a big wringer, two big wooden tubs and a drain in the floor.

Hosiery was first washed in soap flakes and then in rinsing water, and boarded on jumper boards or hap stretchers. Sometimes, garments were set outside to dry, but usually they dried inside Fourteen, which was warm.

White garments were usually smoked with sulphur to make them extra-white. In the back corner of Fourteen was a raised, enclosed little room known as the smoke-box.

Smoke-box instructions: Hang washed and still-wet garments on lines strung across the smoke-box. Place hot coals into the little iron box on the floor and lay your chunks of yellow sulphur right on top of the coals. Close the door and go, leave overnight, and in the morning take your now lovely, soft, white garments, board them and dry them.

N.B. The coals are only supposed to smoulder very gently, not burst into flames! This happened once to Teenie Scollay, Braeside. She panicked, rushed out of Fourteen and around the corner of the next building – right into Mr Adie's arms!

> "What on earth is wrong, Teenie?"
> "Oh, da box is taen fire an Miss Adie'll just *aet* me!"
> "It'll surely not be as bad as all that!"

From about 1930 or so, Peggy Anderson (later Parkin), of Newhouse, spent a lot of her time washing hosiery, and also tweed. Various others helped with this, for example, Sally Couper (aunt of Jim Couper, Seaview.)

Scouring tweed was a heavy job. It had to be washed twice, and then rinsed. The first wash was in soda, which was very hard on the hands. Peggy sometimes came home with her hands bleeding. The second wash was in soap then the wub was rinsed. A long length of wet tweed was difficult to manage even with two people. Often this job would be done by men, or lasses would fetch a weaver or two to give them a hand.

At first, tweed was put through the wringer, but then management decide it shouldn't be wrung. Wet wubs had to be carried in a basket – another heavy job – and pegged up on the drying-green at the back of the picking shed. In winter, a wub sometimes froze to the line!

Peggy once remarked that she seldom got colds. Peter Jamieson assured her, "Hit'll be da sulphur at keeps dem aff o dee!"

Peggy Anderson (Parkin).

The 1930s: Weaving

As tweed production increased, more looms were installed in the old carding-shed. In the mid-30s this building was altered and enlarged to form a big weaving shed. It was more or less built around the carding-shed – which may explain some of the oddities in the weaving-shed floor!

Left to right: Willie Hutchison, Magnie Anderson, John Jamieson, three of the weavers, at the back of the new enlarged weaving shed, late 30s.

Another important development was the introduction of Hattersley "automatic" looms, which were bigger and more complex than the hand-looms. Peter Jamieson, Klonisburn, was the first to use a Hattersley in Voe, after going to weave in Stornoway for a spell. Output was far greater on the automatic loom; 2 x 60 yard wubs a week was normal. The hand-loom was much slower, but some hand-looms were kept in operation, as there were certain patterns that could not be woven on the Hattersley. You could, for example, have single rows of one colour on a hand-loom. The least you could have on an automatic was two rows of one colour.

"Automatic" does not mean what we might expect it to mean nowadays. Far from doing all the work for you, the Hattersley was treadle-driven. If you were not a fit man when you started on this loom, by and by you would certainly be in pretty good shape. Working a treadle loom is like cycling a heavy push-bike all day!

The new weaving shed, with up to fourteen clanking looms in operation, was a noisy place. And very busy: by the late 1930s, they were working 8 am - 8 pm Monday to Friday, and eight hours on Saturday.

The 1930s: "Number Eleven"

Number Eleven staff (plus Jamie Couper) early 1930s, possibly 1931: Back row left to right: Mary Dalziel, Sally Couper, Baabie Balfour, Jamie Couper, Babsy Thomson (of Flett); front row left to right: Lizzie Irvine, Maggie Sutherland, Annie Couper, Olga Comloquoy, Beenie Couper, Teenie Irvine (Tronaster).

Knitwear came a long way in a short time, from the two trainee machine-knitters who started out, to proper factory production.

As with weaving, knitting itself was only part of the process. The ribbed cuffs and neck of a jumper were knitted separately. In the very beginning, these had been hand-knitted, presumably to give the machine-made garment a "hand-made" look, but very soon the cuffs and necks were also machine-made. They then had to be sewn on by hand, stitch for stitch, a painstaking process which left no seam, and was known as "finishing", or "grafting". By the mid-30s there were twenty-two finishers in Number Eleven, as well as ten machinists. There would always be a few staff examining completed garments, labelling, parcelling up orders, and sending out hand-knit orders to women who worked at home.

At this time, all the Number Eleven staff were female. Almost all were young and single. When you married, you left work, looked after your home and took your sock.

Marion Peterson, (later Williamson), Skelberry, came to Number Eleven in 1931 to do finishing. When she started to learn to work a knitting-machine, she was asked to give a guarantee that she would stay at the machine for three years. This was normal practice then. (As time went on, trained machinists who left could take a machine home and continue to work.)

There was no transport for workers in 1931; they had to walk, cycle, or "live-in". During the winter, Marion went to stay in Brungasta, together with other Number Eleven lasses. They shared rooms and ate together in the kitchen. The other side of Brungasta was now occupied by Peter Johnson of Sursetter, the shop manager, and his wife and family. Maggie Johnson would boil tatties for the lasses next door at dinner-time.

Marion Peterson (Williamson).
Courtesy of Marion Williamson

These lasses included Lizzie Peterson from Collafirth, (later Wood, sister to Alex Peterson, Southerhouse), and three Balfour sisters from Grobsness, Alice, Helen and Maggie (later to become Alice Devonald, Helen Williamson and Maggie Brown). With other workers in the house too, it was a lightsome time.

Taken outside Brungasta in the thirties, left to right: Dolly Georgeson, Nesting, Nan Tulloch, Ennisfirth, Maggie Hughson, Nesting, Helen and Alice Balfour, Jessie Johnson, Scord, Muckle Roe. All these lasses worked in number Eleven, apart from Nan who was at Voe House and in the dairy.
Photo courtesy of Chrissie Tait.

Number Eleven staff, left to right: Maggie Sutherland, Lizzie Peterson, Winnie Hall, Maggie Hall, Chrissie Hall, Jessie Hall, Maggie Robertson, Chrissie Nicolson, Annie Williamson, Helen Balfour, Johann Sutherland, Baabie Balfour.

Photo courtesy of Delting History Group.

Left: Osla Hay, formerly shop manager, now hosiery manager in the thirties. She lived at that time in a room in Brungasta, together with other workers. Although she was quite a bit older than most of them, and very much looked up to by most people, she never complained about any noise or fun going on in the house. Right: Ina Sutherland and Maggie Balfour, taken outside Number Eleven in the late thirties.

The Carpenters

The last piece of the business premises to be completed in the 30s was the back wing of Number Eleven, the part nearest the road. This was built after the construction of the weaving shed. There was no need to bring in outside contractors for any of this; Adie's had its own team to do whatever building work was needed.

Jamie Johnson, Kurkigarth, was a stone-mason to trade. He built the Bellevue garden wall out of stones from the old drying-beaches. Chief carpenter was Jerry Hutchison (father of W. Hutchison, Hillend). Jerry was a former ship's carpenter, who had learned his trade in Voe before going to sea. (His first trip was in a sailing vessel.) Another Voe carpenter was Magnie Sutherland (grandfather of Jim Sutherland, Isles Road, and John and Gordon Sutherland, Dale) They were joined by several others, and their base was the Carpenters' Shed, next to the bakery.

The massive pitch-pine timbers in the framing of the Carpenters' Shed were salvaged from the wreck of the *Ayrshire*, a barque of 681 tons wrecked at Gilsa Ayre, Muckle Roe in 1865. She was bound from Quebec to Liverpool with a cargo of timber. (The crew were saved.)

The carpenter squad did varied jobs, e.g. building maintenance, making and repairing bread boxes for the bakery. If there was no wood or construction work to do, they did odd jobs as well; they might be sent to the farm to cure hay or pack wool, for example. But in the late 30s they couldn't have had much time to spare for any of that.

Building Houll: Back, left to right: Mac Brown, Lowrie Umphray, Jamie Johnson (Kurkigarth), Jerry Hutchison. Front: Jamie Couper (Crugan), Johnny Johnson (Hillend), Magnie Sutherland. Photo courtesy of Delting History Group.

Another three houses were built at this time for Adie's workers: Houll, Lyngarth (present day Sjøstua), and Litlatoo. Houll was first occupied in 1937. Lyngarth, built about 1938, was actually built by the firm of Bigland and Mowat. Litlatoo was under construction in 1939.

Houll, just right of centre, was first occupied in 1937. Side view of widden hooses on left. Brungasta beyond them. Rear view of Voe House just above Houll. Far right: lums of Bellevue, with Lower Hillend above. Old Voe Hall appears facing us, at the foot of the Sparl road, on the site of modern Freefield. © Shetland Museum.

Until the end of the Second World War, the carpenters at Voe also made coffins. They made them to size, and kept a stock of what they simply called "coffin wood", ten inches wide, this being considered suitable for the depth of a coffin. To bend it into shape, they would soak it in a big barrel of water. They also kept a stock of name-plates, handles, black cloth to cover the coffin, and a kind of lead to go on the corners.

On the Road

As more and more workers were needed, they came in from Roe, Brae, Nesting and Lunnasting. Those who could not be found accommodation had to cycle, or walk. And walk they did if they had to, five, six, seven miles, morning and night, at least in summer-time. Sixteen-year-old Maggie Ann Williamson, Skelberry, (later Couper), joined other Lunnasting walkers for the summer of 1932, until she was able to get a cycle. Then, in the winter of '32, vans were laid on to fetch workers and it became a routine to cycle in summer, and go by van in winter. By and by, the vans ran all year round.

Gideon Hall from Roe had been driving to Adie's for some time before he moved his family to the newly-built house of Houll in October 1937. Like John Wood and Erty Hughson (Maurice Hughson's grandfather), he did bread deliveries, he picked up shop supplies in Lerwick, (essential now that the steamer no longer called at Voe), he might drive the selling van, and he always did morning and night runs with workers. These were to Nesting, Lunnasting or the turntable above the Roe Brig. No four-wheeled vehicles at that time could pass over the Roe brig except peerie cars, like Doctor Hendry's, for example, and if he stopped in the middle he couldn't get out!

**Gideon Hall. © Ramsay.
Photo courtesy of Jean Hall.**

This looks more like a truck than a van, but it may be a "soft-top" van without the soft top! The Roe workers heading home, Gideon Hall driving, 1930s. From left: Andrew J. Johnson, Leebie Williamson, Jarm Robertson, Katie Johnson, Maggie Johnson, Winnie Hall, Maggie Robertson, Mootie Williamson, Jerry Williamson, Chrissie Hall, Ruby Johnson.   Photo courtesy of Andy Robertson.

Van-drivers became eart-kent. Much could be written about them. They drove fairly large vehicles, often packed with people, on poor roads, at all times of the year. They were on the road early and were the last of the staff to finish at night. They were endlessly obliging – "sent errands" were an understood part of the job. And, in the days when hardly anyone had a car, and buses were few, they provided a very useful transport service for lots of people. Their routes were known and never varied. They would give you a lift without question. With a bit of planning, things could be arranged…

For example, John Wood's peat banks were beside the Vidlin road. Other Voe folk also had peats out this way. So on a suitable evening, he was very likely to have a lot of extra passengers on his six o'clock night run to Vidlin. John would drop them all off at their peat banks, go home with the Vidlin workers, come back and raise his own peats for a couple of hours. When he went home, everyone else went too!

Years and years later, when John's grandson, John Thompson, shop assistant in the late 60s, was driving the selling van to Gonfirth, the system still worked. "Boy, wid du set aff dis tushkar an spade up at my paet bank? Hit's hard ta kerry dem on da motor-bike!"

Shopping

What could you buy at Voe?

Quite a lot. Every necessity in the food line. Paraffin for lamps. Tar for roofs. Creosote. Hens' meal and corn. Nails, steeples, paint and putty. Rope, various thicknesses. Everything needed to maintain push bikes. Buttons, needles, thread and mackin wires. Fishing line and hooks. Etc, etc, etc. Tobacco. Whisky. Beer, which was cask beer, bottled in the back shop, (108 x 5-gill bottles to the barrel). They bottled stout too, but it was popular mainly at peat-casting time.

And upstairs, there was a selection of drapery – hats, coats, skirts, frocks, etc. There was one side room with a stock of shoes, and another with crockery. Every year, before Christmas, Jessie would set out a display of items for presents. It was not often that anybody could go to shop in Lerwick.

So you could buy many things in Voe, but if there was something special you really needed, you could always send an errand to Lerwick or Scalloway with a helpful van driver …

Conversation in the bakery despatch room:

> Jamie Couper: Jóhn, dis is an errand at Maggie Sutherland is needin dee ta get her in Scallowa.

John Wood: (reading) Two invincible hard hats - whaar ta da deevil will I get dem?

J.C.: (looking over John's shoulder) Na, it can't be dat! No, no, sees du, hit's two invisible hair nets!

J.W.: Invisible hair nets? Weel, if dey're invisible, foo ta hell will I ken if I'm gotten dem or no?

Mutton Supply

In the 30s, Adie's sold a lot of fresh mutton (or as we would say nowadays, lamb!) to customers in the south, some quite far away down in England. This went on until the wartime, though obviously not all year round. Magnie Manson remembered well how the system worked.

It depended on two things, the mail delivery and the departure of the steamer from Lerwick. Wednesday was a steamer day. Late on Tuesday, Adie's mailbag, and any meat orders it contained, had to be fetched from town. Otherwise, the orders would not have arrived till Wednesday, which was too late. The required number of lambs were slaughtered on Tuesday night. (Adie's farm obviously produced lambs, but many were bought in.)

Peter Johnson, pictured here with his wife, Maggie Irvine, was always known as "Peter o Sursetter", though he spent more of his life in Brungasta. His entire working life, outwith his war service, was spent in Adie's shop. He was working there before he went to the First World War in 1915. Wounded at Passchendaele, he was invalided out of the army and sent to work on a farm near Dornoch before the war's end. Then he returned to the shop, finally leaving at the age of 70, having worked part-time for five years. Peter and Maggie married in 1926. She also had worked at Voe, in Adie's post office, about 1916/17, before she joined the WRNS. Their family, Joyce, Drewie and Betty, all worked at Voe at various times.   Photo courtesy of Betty Sutherland.

Early on Wednesday morning, the carcasses were cut up in the back shop by Peter Johnson, with Mr. Adie reading out orders and two men sewing up mutton joints in straw bags. A van would then deliver the shipment to the Wednesday steamer.

It was a very early start on Wednesday – five in the morning. There was a special "alarm clock" at Brungasta: Andy Couper the baker, who started work at four, would always rattle a stone along Peter Johnson's window as he passed by heading for the bakery!

Denner Time

One thing Adie's never did was provide meals. Tea breaks were taken on the premises, but at dinner-time the place shut down. Those who lived nearby went home for dinner, and everybody else made arrangements to eat at someone's house – someone who was a capable cook, didn't live too far away, and was willing to have you! Many housewives made dinners for workers. Annie Hall, once she got established in her new home at Houll, usually cooked for eight or nine.

It was another Adie's routine, folk walking in groups for their dinner, and it continued long after the war. Some went as far as the Hoga (Betty Anderson's), or round the banks to Hillcrest (Katie Johnson's). It was a chance to stretch your legs, get some fresh air, and meet people who didn't do the same work as you – it could be quite sociable. Johnny Brown, the van driver, might even have time to pock a troot in the Fusselburn!

Fitba

Among the men who had come to Adie's from the south, there were several keen football players, such as the weaver John Dawson and baker Willie Hughes. They started up football sessions and got a lot of local young men interested. There was no absolutely flat ground suitable to play on, but one or two places could be used. The Hestafields were popular, and an area near the present-day kirk.

Johnny Hughson, uncle of Maurice Hughson. The house in the background seems to be the old house of the Garths, just north by Sursetter.

Bright lights and Batteries

There was electricity at Adie's long before the days of the Hydro Board, in fact, before the Second World War. Ted Adie acquired a diesel generator, (probably from Sir Arthur Nicolson of Fetlar), and this provided lighting for the business premises, Voe House and Bellevue.

It was probably 1934. Joyce and Drewie Johnson, the Brungasta bairns, were taken down to the shop specially to see these new-fangled lights. Ruby Anderson of the Hoga remembers too, as a peerie lass, being shown how the switch on the shop wall would bring the lights on. It must have seemed quite a novelty, and not just to the bairns.

The generator stood in the peerie shed adjoining Fourteen, next to the garages. It seems to have been installed by Macleod and Macleans. As well as producing electricity, it could also charge wet-cell batteries. From miles around, people sent their run-down wireless batteries to Voe, and every night, Gideon Hall would charge up a bank of batteries to be picked up, or delivered by van, the next day.

And so...the Thirties ended

The bakery had felt the effects of the Depression of the early Thirties more than other parts of the business. For a while there may only have been three bakers. Johnny Johnson of Hillend had gone to sea for a time and Lowrie Brown went a season or two to the whaling. Robbie Jamieson had gone to work in tweed. Later on, however, things picked up and Johnny and Lowrie were both back in the bakery.

Tweed was on overtime, Number Eleven was packed out, and the third new house in as many years, Litlatoo, was up to the waa-heads, when war was declared in September 1939.

Men in the RNR or the

Dodie Johnson in uniform.

Territorial Army would leave at once for war service. They were followed in October 1939 by the "first militia", all men 21 years of age. This included Dodie Johnson, Hillend, from the weaving-shed.

Chapter 4
Wartime

Business carried on at Adie's in the wartime, but the war brought many changes. A steady stream of staff were called up to serve in the armed forces – first men, then later women too. Rations came in, affecting most of the shop stock and petrol.

Ted Adie had to spend much of his time in Lerwick, as he now became second in command of what was eventually known as the Home Guard. (He had been a Lieutenant in the First World War and was now promoted to Major.) In addition, he was Convenor of the County Council from 1938-1945. His eldest brother, James, who had left Shetland in 1922, returned now, and was sometimes at Voe, but the family lived in Lerwick, as he and his Norwegian wife, the former Hanka Lange, were heavily involved in the reception of Norwegian refugees.

Early in the war, Shetland was seen as a likely target for invasion, and British forces poured in. The RAF became well established in Graven, where Sullom Voe had been a flying-boat base from the first days of the war. Three army camps were built in Voe, one beside the kirk, one in the lower Hillend toon, and one at the Loch. The Voe Hall, (on the site of modern-day Freefield), was taken over by the army. So was one half of the old post office building, across the road from the shop. This was used as a kind of office. It was here that any soldier had to come if he was "on a charge" for some misdeed or other!

Work had to stop on the building of Litlatoo. It was given a temporary corrugated iron roof and used as an army telephone exchange.

The new house of Lyngarth next door had been built for Johnny Hughson (shop assistant) and Lizzie Irvine (Number Eleven), who had recently married and moved in. It was now commandeered for officer accommodation and Johnny Hughson was very shortly called up.

Curfews, passwords and gas masks became everyday things.

The Shop in Wartime

Just ower fifty year ago,
 Ahint da coonter in Lower Voe,
Tree young smashers did da wark -
Mary, Bertha, an Bella Clark!
   (from Peter and Bella's Golden Wedding Song!)

Bertha Wood and Bella Clark.
Photo courtesy of Bella Hughson.   **Mary Leask and Bella Clark**

In 1940 Johnny Hughson and his brother Peter, both shop staff, were called up. Jessie Nicolson was about to marry Bertie Couper, Hamars, and leave the job she had held for fifteen years. Within the space of a couple of summer months, three new shop lasses were taken on: Mary Leask from Girlsta, Bella Clark, Tarrarit, Vidlin, and Bertha Wood of the widden hooses, daughter of van driver John Wood. The shop manager continued to be Peter Johnson, Brungasta. His son Drewie would join the shop staff in 1943 when he left school.

Despite rationing, life was very busy in the shop. The forces created extra business and rations created extra chores. Ration coupons had to be checked carefully and cut out. All bulk supplies were normally weighed up and packed on the premises but now often had to be made up in suitable ration-sizes.

Shop hours were 8 am to 7 pm with an hour for dinner and a break from 5 pm to 5.30 pm for tea. Thursday was the shop half-day. Many of Adie's workers arrived in the morning, as they had always done, with an errand line to be made ready for their homeward trip at night. Maybe one for their next door neighbours as well. It was normal practice for a pillowcase or flour bag to be left to hold the shopping. "Reeky" houses were fairly obvious by the scent of the bag!

The shop van continued its rounds, visiting Collafirth, Dale and Grobsness, with a driver and a shop assistant. The folk from Hubansetter and Queenster walked over the hill to Gonfirth to meet the van. When snow blocked the road to Collafirth, the old Collafirth women would walk out to the Berry Knowe, with kishies and flour bags on their backs. They seemed to look on this as a great fun!

Flour was bought by the bowe (boll), or half-bowe. Folk would send in an order and the van would deliver. It never seemed to be in short supply, though at one time it was brown in colour.

Plenty of other things were in short supply, especially as the war wore on. A well-known character from the north valley exploded one day in the shop, "Good God, what is dis world comin tae? Can't even get a god-damned match! Dey'll be stoppin da breath o life next!"

Tea, sugar, butter, margarine, jam, bacon, meat and many other things were rationed. Sweeties were rare, as was fruit. When fruit did come in, it was allocated to bairns or pregnant mothers. (How was a shop assistant supposed to know if a woman was pregnant? Answer; it was officially written in the back of her ration book. Too bad for anyone who wanted to keep it quiet!)

Bread was rationed in B. U.s (Bread Units). A recurring complaint in Collafirth was "Boy, I hae nae mair o yon bloody Bay-Yews!"

Beer was available in wartime, but spirits were hard to obtain. If any whisky did come in, Peter Johnson tended to lay it aside upstairs in the room that once held shoes for sale. He wanted every man in the place to be able to have a bottle of whisky at Christmas, and stockpiled until he had enough. A name was carefully written on each bottle. (Any household without a man could also have a bottle, if they so wished!)

Margarine seemed to be more readily available than some other items. Bella faithfully made up a grocery order every week for a Girlsta customer, including a pound of margarine. Eventually, the order was revised, with the instruction "Please send no more margarine. My drawers are full of it".

Clothes, by and by, became unobtainable, and the stocks in the upstairs shop disappeared. It was still possible to buy a length of material, using clothing coupons, and make your own. Mary Leask, who was a skilled dressmaker, often made clothes out of flour bags. The material was good strong cotton, but the snag was the huge blue and red letters "PAUL'S BEST" stencilled across the bags. It was Bertha Wood's mother, Annie, who hit upon a method of removing the lettering, and after that, many a garment was sewn out of flour bags, and dyed a suitable colour. An Air Force parachute, when you could get one, provided silk for nighties and underwear.

The Bakery in Wartime

The Voe bakery was very busy throughout the war; it supplied bread to all the forces from Girlsta and north, as well as the local folk. Bakery workers were normally exempt from call-up, but there was such a demand that army bakers were brought in to supplement the staff. The bakers normally started work at 4 am, but at the height of wartime production they started at 2 am and worked two shifts.

The teenage Andy Robertson, from Knowe, Muckle Roe, arrived at Voe in 1940, and after a week or two in the picking shed, he was transferred to the bakery despatch room until his own call-up in 1943. The bakers at that time were Willie Cochrane, foreman, from Alyth, Perthshire, Lowrie Brown, Johnny Johnson, young Andy Wood, and Andy Couper of the widden hooses. There were also several army bakers, who varied.

The best-remembered of the army bakers seem to be Tommy Ashley from Shropshire, and the Tynesider Tommy Elsie. Tommy Elsie was a lively character whose exploits included building a canoe, out of wood and flour bags covered with coats of paint. He regularly went for a swim off the pier, even in winter. His footprints sometimes formed a trail in the snow from the bakery to the sea! Then he'd come in and dry off by the oven.

Another soldier baker was "old Angus". It was difficult to look him in the eye, as his eyes looked outwards in opposite directions.

In the despatch room were Jamie Couper, Hamars, and Andy, with extra helpers often brought in because they were so busy. Young Jamie Johnson of Kurkigarth and Jamie Clark of Tarrarit were among those who worked here for a time. Neither of them was the one that was so vyndless that every time he was sent for water from the well he came back soaking!

A wartime group. Back: Jamie Johnson, Kurkigarth, (despatch room). Middle row, left to right: Joyce Johnson, Brungasta (office), Drewie Johnson, Brungasta (shop), Mary Leask (van). Front row, left to right: Miss Fulton, (office), Jamie Couper, (despatch room), Bertha Wood, (shop).

Stocks of flour never ran out, but there was no proper fat to be had. Something called "emulsion" was used. There was no shortage of local eggs, bartered for groceries at the shop or the van. The bakery used them and preserved any surplus in waterglass.

Vanloads of bread and biscuits went out every day, and in addition, trucks would arrive to fetch supplies for the forces. On a warm summer's day it was sometimes a problem getting the bread to cool properly before despatch. It would be set outside in large quantities, and a careful eye had to be kept on teefy sheep!

A man's job?

> When we guid an telled Miss Adie at we wid go inta da weaving-shed, she took a laachin! She laached an laached till da taers ran doon her face. We never usually saw her even smilin. Weel, we never kent what ta dö, so ta feenish up wi, we just laached tö!
>
> *(Babs Sutherland/ Robertson)*

Up and down the length of Britain, women in wartime were taking on jobs that had always been done by men.

At Voe, several lasses were transferred from Number Eleven into the weaving shed – Babs and Gracie Sutherland of Skelberry, Vidlin, Joann Sutherland of the Old Schoolhouse and Winnie Hall from Roe. The few men left weaving did not all approve of this development; one was heard to comment "Dey will be no paece noo!" However, after the initial shock, there was no problem, the lasses were well treated, and given any help they needed to become proficient on the loom. Other lasses would later follow them.

Mootie Couper (later Gray), of the widden hooses, learned to warp, and worked alongside Jamie Tulloch, (South Voxter). Chrissie Nicolson (later Tait), of Scarvataing, Aith, who had been working since about 1936 in Number 11, worked as a baker for a time.

Chrissie Nicolson (Tait) who went on to become a baker in the forces.
Photo courtesy of Chrissie Tait

These lasses were not all to stay for the whole of the war, as women became liable to call-up. Babs and Gracie, for example, ended up in munitions work in Manchester making Rolls-Royce Merlin engines.

Several van-drivers were called up, one after another – Johnny Brown, Kirkhouse, Joseph Hutchison, Newhouse, and Thomas John Thompson, Setter. John Wood and Gideon Hall drove throughout the war; Peter Jamieson would come from the loom if they were stuck for a driver. And in 1943, Mary Leask, by then Mrs Dodie Johnson, learned to drive a van and drove till the end of the war.

Mary's driving lessons, from John Wood and Peter Jamieson, were all pretty straightforward, like the first one: she sat by John Wood's side as he drove to Aith, and then John said "Now, du tak her back!"

The roads at this time were mostly untarred single-track; there was no tar, but no traffic either. Bits of the main road were tarred. There weren't any crash-barriers, of course. Grobsness was probably the worst road to drive, "but Collafirth wisna great!" (Mary)

Mary did bread delivery runs three times a week to the NAAFI at Sullom Voe, with a stop along a Church of Scotland canteen near the present junction to Sellaness. She had a pass to allow her into the RAF camp, which seemed just like a town, with all the various huts and buildings. On one occasion she took Bella and Bertha with her to see the camp. They were stopped at the gate and the other two had to wait in the guardhouse till Mary came back out again!

Mary Leask, now Johnson, wartime van driver.

Soldiers

> When da Air Force cam to stay
> I'd my curlers in all day.... *(post-war song)*

In the wartime, uniformed men were everywhere. Some were local boys home on welcome spells of leave. (In the early war years, when invasion was so much feared, any returning soldier had to take home his full kit, including his rifle.) There were also the many servicemen, from all parts of Britain, who were stationed in the area. Most were well-accepted, many made friends and would regularly visit local families. Annie Wood even washed bakery aprons for the "two Tommies" who worked with Andy, her son.

Contact with the visitors gave local folk an insight into war conditions in other parts of the country. One of the army bakers, for example, was a Londoner who lost seven members of his family in one night of bombing.

Social life was not lacking in the war years. Dances were held quite frequently, even though the forces had to get late passes and everybody was supposed to carry a gas mask. Individual regiments would hold dances of their own in the Mossbank Hall, the Brae Hall and the Voe Hall, which were all used by the army anyway.

Local bairns walked past the Voe Hall, and an army camp, every day on their way to and from school – bairns like Myra Anderson of the Hoga (later Irvine), and her brother and sisters. They were on good terms with the soldiers, and were often invited in to see films in the hall. They also saw ENSA entertainers like George Formby and Gracie Fields, two of the best-known stage stars of the day. Gracie apparently paid a visit to Adie's weaving shed, which caused a bit of excitement.

Among the hundreds of British army personnel, there were inevitably one or two renegades. Once a soldier tried to break into the back shop, and bent the barrel of his rifle on the bars across the window. Another became known as "Da Rhuburb Fusilier", after he fell by drunk among the Brungasta rhubarb, rifle and all. He was duly recovered by somebody from the camp.

And there was Muirhead, who indulged in a little black-marketeering. He pinched a stock of long-johns from the army store at the Loch of Voe camp, and sold them around the place. However, one local man must have regretted his bargain buy. It was quickly recorded in verse that:

> *so-and-so* can pass da cars
> Steppin along in Muirhead's draaers!

Occasionally, a hired car would arrive at the shop with a load of Norwegians from Lunna, come to buy whatever alcohol they could find or the ingredients for home brew. They always seemed to have been drinking; people found it hard to understand. These were the "Shetland Bus" men, who would be famous in later years, all on active service and engaged in very dangerous work. They were given priority by the Ordnance Corps above all other forces in Shetland for the provision of arms and equipment. Owing to wartime secrecy, few people at the time really knew very much about them at all, and anyone who did, couldn't say.

The Lofty Heights of Gonfirth

> Our section is comprised from Voe
> Of men adept to meet the foe
> And they in twos each night do go
> To guard the Heights of Gonfirth
>
> *(from poem by M. Anderson)*

The poem, like much else, was made up for fun. The whole idea of the Home Guard nowadays is likely to raise a smile, thanks to the well-loved TV classic "Dad's Army". And no doubt there was many a laugh to be had, and many a yarn to be told.

But it wasn't such a joke at the time, particularly in the early war years, when the rapid German occupation of Denmark and Norway made Shetland seem a likely next target. The islands must have felt very vulnerable. There was no shortage of men volunteering to take part in home defence. Over a thousand men enrolled in the Local Defence Volunteers, which would later be known as the Home Guard.

> **Local skyimp:** What does L. D. V. staand for, dan?
> - Look, Dook an Vanish!

All the things we have heard about were probably true, especially in the early days: drill with broom handles, (and apparently, at least one tushkar), one rifle between ten, uniforms all one size, etc. etc. The personnel were either too old or too young for call-up, exempt, or in a reserved occupation. But there they were, often from the word go. "Some guid intil it right awey." A man being called up to join the forces, if he had first been in the Home Guard, had the right to go away in uniform, as Willie Hutchison of Hillend did.

There were handy instructors for all necessary skills, among the army right on the doorstep. Some of the young officers felt a certain diffidence in training First World War veterans. "Look at that man there. He was all through the First War. What can I teach him?"

Training sessions, night excursions and look-out duty – yes, the Heights of Gonfirth! Explosives, sabotage, etc, etc. Most Voe employees knew that the Home Guard had some kind of store in the old post office building. Everybody knew they went up to the top of Gonfirth every night. Nobody knew, until the war had finished, that they also had a hideout in the Fillarönies, where they had kept explosives and other equipment, so that this could have been a base for resistance in the event of invasion. A sobering thought.

Another sobering thought for younger folk: the amount of planes going over. They were sometimes heard and not seen, but there were always planes. Bairns going to school quickly learned to distinguish the sound of German planes, and knew when to hide in ditches. People never knew what was going on, not even on the day when the despatch room boys stood at the door and tried to count the aircraft overhead. They couldn't; there were too many. And on one memorable day, in the early war years, all Home Guard members of Adie's staff were actually sent home to stand by.

The picture shows some of the members of the Voe Home Guard. There were a good few more who are not in the picture.

Taken very early in the war. Back, L. to R. Gideon Hall, Houll, Andy Couper, widden hooses, Sergeant McLaughlin (?), Magnus Thompson, Setter, John Wood. Front, Peter Johnson, Brungasta, Atty Wood, widden hooses, Johnny Johnson, Hillend, Fraser Sinclair, Sandness, who worked in the office, Johnny Hughson, widden hooses, Willie Hutchison, Hillend.   **Photo courtesy of Bella Hughson.**

The Home Guard was once given the task of getting through the security at RAF Sullom Voe, and, apparently, was remarkably successful. They got in quite easily, tied labels on to everything in sight, (including, it is said, the rifle of a sleeping guard), and went home again. There was, allegedly, "hell to pay" at Sullom Voe!

At last

The war with Germany ended in May 1945, but the fighting in the Far East still went on. Johnny Brown, home on leave from the RAF in August, was about to be posted to Okinawa, south of the Japanese mainland.

True to form, the evening before he was due to go, Johnny was up in the Kirkhouse garage doing engine repairs with Magnus Thompson of Setter, who was also home on leave. His wife Maggie, (formerly Maggie Balfour), was at home in the widden hooses with their infant daughter, Kathleen, when she heard the news that Japan had surrendered and the war was finally won. She was wild with joy. "I ran! I ran every fit up da rodd ta tell Johnny!"

He would still have to go away, but the war was over.

Johnny Brown.

Chapter 5
Postwar

Back to Normality?

So the war was over at last. You could tear down the blackout curtains straight away, and take the covers off the headlights on the vans and the motorbikes. You could forget about passwords and gas masks and start to live without constant worry. The huge relief was only matched by the longing to get back to some kind of normality. In practice this took time. And perhaps, life could never be quite the same again anyway.

Some loved and familiar faces were missing. Servicemen and seamen began returning from all parts of the world with varying experiences of the war, some quite horrendous, which might or might not be told at some time. The army camps and RAF Sullom Voe gradually emptied and closed, reducing local employment. Former employ-

Some Adie's workers about 1946. Left to right: Jamie Johnson, Kurkigarth, Johann Williamson, Uphouse, Skelberry, Drewie Johnson, Brungasta, Gracie Sutherland, Skelberry.
Photo courtesy of Babs Robertson.

A bigger group from the same time, about 1946. Faces from left to right: Teenie Irvine, Tronaster, Babs Sutherland, Skelberry, Johann Williamson, Drewie Johnson, Jessie Johnson, Roe (probably), Maggie Herculeson, Newhouse, Skelberry, Jamie Johnson, Maggie Ann Williamson, Uphouse, Skelberry, Joan Thomson, Horn, Vidlin, Gracie Sutherland.
Photo courtesy of Babs Robertson.

ees came back to Adie's in need of work and a real effort was made to take them all back on.

There was an outbreak of weddings in the years just after the war. The new brides stopped work and became housewives. It was recognised by everybody that their place was now in the home. The post-war baby-boom was shortly in full swing.

Voe about 1950. Uppermost on left is the original house of Skol. Bottom left: the old manse (shortly to be replaced by Fagradal), then Lyngarth (now Sjøstua) and Litlatoo.
© Ratter. Courtesy of Wilma Couper.

Rationing, to everyone's dismay, dragged on for years, and many things continued to be in short supply. When Bella Clark married Peter Hughson in 1946, there were two wedding dresses to choose from in the Lerwick shops. Mary Johnson's dressmaking skills were called upon for a long time after the war's end. She lost count of the number of wedding dresses she made.

Johnny and Lizzie Hughson were at last able to live in Lyngarth. Next door, the corrugated iron sheets were removed from Litlatoo and the house was completed by Adie's carpenter squad – Archie Johnson of Hillcrest, John Wood of Sullom (father of Lottie Hall, Isles Road), Jerry Hutchison and others.

There was a demand for housing everywhere, and in the years 1949-50 the first council houses in Voe, the Cruden houses at Isles Road, were occupied, mostly by Adie's workers. Some of them moved from one or two rooms in the old widden hooses into what must have seemed like a palace at the time – a three-bedroomed house with a bathroom! Among the first to move into the Crudens were Andy Robertson and Babs Sutherland, who had married in 1948.

Myra I.C. Adie, known as Miss Adie, eldest of the eleven children of William and Margaret Adie. To her brothers and sisters she was Myra, but to her nieces and nephews she was always Aunt Mona. Photo courtesy of J. A. Adie.

As the widden hooses emptied they were demolished, one by one. Adie's then built the present house of Burnside, roughly on the site.

Miss Adie, now well over seventy, was able to take a less active part in the business after the war. She did, together with her sister Mrs Hamilton, continue to take an active part in running Voe House and its staff, and organising the produce of the dairy and the garden.

The Norwegian Connection

Hardly a summer day passes by without a photo being taken from the Hillend corner, looking down to the sea. It's the postcard view of Voe, and many people think it reminds them of somewhere in Norway. And it does have a Norwegian connection.

James Adie, oldest brother of Ted Adie, was married to Hanka Lange, daughter of Alexander Lange of Sandefjord in Norway. Alexander Lange was a pioneer figure in the Norwegian whaling industry, and at one time he was manager of the Olna whaling station. James and Hanka Adie returned from North Berwick to Shetland in the wartime, where they were put in charge of a refugee camp for Norwegians fleeing the German occupation of Norway. By the end of the war 3000 people had passed through the camp. The work they did was very much appreciated. Hanka Adie also taught Norwegian evening classes in Lerwick, which were in demand.

Two of their family later became managers in the firm: Esme Bennett and James A. Adie.

In 1948 the original house of Skol was built, for Mrs Bennett, who was a widow with a young son. She had set her heart on this house, and had even begun to dig out the foundations, when Johnny Brown saw what she was at, and stopped along to tell her, "You shouldna be doin dis yourself!" Next day there were ten men with spades and shovels to help. Skol created a great deal of interest, as it was a real Norwegian house, very likely the first in Shetland. The logs came over from Norway, accompanied by a Norwegian builder. People still remember him; he may even have played the accordion at some local function. Together with Archie Johnson and others in the carpenters' squad, he put up this strange new house. We can imagine the speculation! Not only were the walls made of wood, but they were going to cover the roof with nothing less than *poans* (turf)! "Weel, dat will never wirk here!" "Ever did you hear da laek?"

The poans on the roof were actually not a success, and were eventually replaced, but the house of Skol certainly added to the "Norwegian" appearance of Voe. So did Mrs Bennett herself, on a snowy winter's day, ski-ing.

Shop and Office

Adie's main office, right next to the shop, looked after the books, wages and mail, and dealt with all phone enquiries and messages. In the forties and fifties, there were usually two office staff. When Ruby Anderson of Hoga arrived as a school-leaver in 1947, Jamie Couper, Hamars, had transferred from the bakery despatch room only a few months before. Jamie had been learning the ropes from Fraser Sinclair, a Sandness man who had been a mainstay in the office both before and after his war service, but who was now leaving to take over a shop in Sandness.

Ruby had been told by her commercial course teacher that nowhere in Shetland would any of the class ever find an office system as good as the one they had been taught in school. They were simply not to expect it. She was surprised to find that her teacher was wrong; Adie's system was very good. They also had the very latest technology, a Royal typewriter with "magic margins", something else she had been using at school but told not to expect! Another innovation was an adding machine, forerunner of the calculator, though not pocket-size! (It could add up to a million pounds, and did, several times, but only for the fun of it!) By 1950, they also had an internal telephone system, installed by James A. Adie. This Ruby felt to be a great boon, and saved many a trip through the rain.

It was very busy at Voe. There was still very little personal or public transport, so every morning three van-drivers, John Wood, Gideon Hall and Johnny Brown, were still setting off in all directions to fetch workers. Seating in the vans, (as all their former passengers remember only too well!), was just

**Ruby Anderson (Johnson) © Ramsay.
Photo courtesy of Ruby Johnson.**

wooden forms, removed when they got back to Voe so the vans could then be used for selling, bread delivery or fetching supplies.

It wasn't just the firm that was busy. The Voe quarry had re-opened after the war when the Kames was being tarred. The pier was busy with fishing-boats landing catches; Ruby remembers as many as fifteen boats at one time. It all made for a buzz of activity and plenty of trade for the shop.

Just as before, the shop was, in many ways, the hub of everything. Behind the counter were rows of hooks bearing keys with large brass numbered keyfobs – one for each of the buildings, returned there every night. The shop provided items for every part of the business, charging everything carefully up to the appropriate department. The shop ran the fuel pump. The shop made up boxes and bags of groceries for workers to take home. It supplied fishing boats. It stocked up and sent out the selling van. And it was, of course, a social meeting place.

The shop, as many people still remember it, had a counter round three sides of it, and was shelved right to the high ceiling. Nobody ever seemed to use a step-ladder; there was a splendid system for getting items off the high shelves. Bairns like Kathleen Brown found it quite fascinating. Every time you went to the shop you hoped somebody would ask for a bottle of lemonade from the highest shelf, or even a jar of jam, which was fairly high up too. The vital piece of equipment was an old wooden staff, and the maneouvre was: with the staff in the right hand, *cleek* the item off the shelf, and with the left hand, *catch*! This must have taken a bit of training to master, but nobody ever saw a broken lemonade bottle! (Interestingly, in the back shop, where the alcohol was kept, step-ladders were used. Perhaps the price affected the risks?)

Myra Anderson (Irvine).
Photographer: E. Sinclair
Photo courtesy of Tina Johnson.

The number of shop staff remained at four. When Myra Anderson, Ruby's sister, arrived in 1951, Peter Johnson, Brungasta, was shop manager, with Peter Hughson, Leonard Anderson of Gruttin and Myra. Davie Anderson from Aith returned to the shop from his National Service as Leonard departed to do his.

National Service had become a new part of life and all young men had to go and do their stint. It was compulsory, but it could be flexible, for example, Jamie Hutchison of Hillend deferred his until he had finished his apprenticeship as a warper/weaver.

Tweed – the busiest ever

Tony Herculson at work in T.M. Adie's warping shed. c. late 1950s. © Shetland Museum

When Jamie Hutchison began his apprenticeship in 1947, he started by warping tweed with Jarm Robertson, Knowe, Muckle Roe, who like so many others had recently returned from the war. At first they set up the warp on stakes, in the ootbye area of the picking shed but by the end of the 40s, a warping-mill was installed in the old garage right next door (the former gun-shed).

A completed warp was wound on to a big spool which then had to be set on the back of a loom and every individual strand of yarn separately threaded into place in preparation for weaving. Standard weight tweed had 672 warp threads – it was very easy to get one wrong!

Tweed was very busy after the war, and got still busier. When Tammy Robertson of Quam started windin pirms in 1946, the weaving shed was full of men (and women, too, for a time – Babs and Gracie Sutherland returned to the loom after the war). Most weavers produced at least two 60-yard wubs each week on the Hattersley looms. There were always a few on handlooms which were much slower, but which still needed the warp set up on stakes in the old-fashioned way.

As time went on, more and more weavers worked at home. There were also some weavers in Scalloway, including John Jamieson, who used to weave at Voe, and Willie Sutherland (father of Larry Sutherland, Scalloway). Warps were spooled up and delivered to them all by the van drivers.

Two warpers were needed to keep the weavers going. Tony Herculson from Nesting also did warping in Voe for a while, and Pete Blance, now of Houll, Voe, was taken on straight from school in 1955, at the height of production, when they were having to warp nine wubs a day. Pete really wanted to be a weaver, so he was disappointed when he had to learn to warp. Tony Herculson, who was to train him, was also disappointed, as his last trainee had felt the same!

Magnie Anderson, Hoga, at the loom in the late 1950s. Behind him could be Magnie Manson, Pund.
© Shetland Museum.

Pete Blance's job interview (fairly typical of others):

    Major Adie: When do you leave school?... What would you like to do?

    P.B.:   I think I'd like to be a weaver.

    M.A.:   There'll be a job for you!

A group of weavers in the mid-fifties. L. to R., Henry Hunter, Nesting, Magnus Thompson, Setter, Magnie Tait, Gonfirth, Jamie Hutchison, Hillend, Jerry Williamson, Roe, Billy Georgeson, Vidlin (?). Photo courtesy of Hazel Hutchison.

Andy Robertson, back home from the Navy, came to work in tweed after a few years back in the bakery despatch room. He didn't care for weaving, but warping was all right. He also worked a lot with Johnny Hughson, another ex-Navy man, keeping tweed operations going smoothly.

Ootbye in the picking shed they had a blackboard with the names of all the weavers who worked for Adie's, both on and off the premises. Andy remembers as many as thirty-two names on this list. Alongside the names they would write who was weaving what wub, and for which customer, who was needing a new warp sent, and so on.

Meanwhile, round the corner of the weaving shed... left to right: Tony Herculson, Willie Hall, Roe, Andy Robertson, Tammy Hall, Roe. Tammy worked in the despatch room, the others in tweed.
Photo courtesy of Hazel Hutchison.

Warps went to weavers and came back as wubs to be greasy-mended, scoured, clean-mended and sent to the customer.

What Andy enjoyed most was baling and shipping out the finished tweed. A bale consisted of six wubs, wrapped in tar paper and finally hessian, sewn up tightly. Many customers' names became very familiar and it was very interesting to think of all the different places the tweed went. A great deal of it (90% in 1955) went to America: e.g. "HILTON, Boston, Mass." A lot of small orders went to Italy e.g. jacket lengths, and short lengths for making caps. Lightweight tweed to Japan. A black and white check for Christian Dior.

Once the bales were ready, Gideon Hall would collect them with the Voe van, and away they went to the North boat, and further by British Road Services.

In 1956, mains electricity reached Voe. The big warping-mill became motorised, making it easier for one man to use. The local doctor, Doctor Porter, looked along one day to see this new development. He took it all in, nodded and commented, "All very fine, but it'll need fewer men now!"

It was not electricity, however, that started the run-down. It was nothing less than the collapse of the American market, when a quota system brought in by the U.S. government strictly limited the import of woollen fabrics to the States.

1955 was about as good as it got.

Tweed kept going for a long time, but it was less busy and Pete Blance never did learn to weave. A couple of years later, he was transferred to Number Eleven.

Picking Shed lasses

Warping, like weaving, was usually a man's job but could be done by women: Joann Johnson, Ness, Weathersta (later Irvine) did warping for handlooms for a time. Picking tweed, however, was commonly done by women, though men would also pick tweed at times.

There might usually be three or four lasses in the picking shed, poised on high stools at the long, smooth table, clicking scissors and wielding tweezers, and each rolling a wub across the table top. Someone was always sitting on the "perch" before the window, looking for the knots in a hanging wub with the aid of the daylight behind it. Once found, knots were pulled through to one side of the wub ready for greasy-mending, when these knots and other imperfections would be sorted out. There was always that smell with the greasy wubs, not unpleasant, but just …greasy! Washed tweed smelt clean, felt soft, and had shrunk quite a bit since the first time you saw it. Clean-mending a light-coloured wub, especially a check or a marl, was a picnic. It mostly amounted to trimming off ends and you could feel sorry for the poor soul next to you with her nose into black or dark green, tweezing out every little speck of fluff or particle of stray thread or, goodness knows, heather root or whatever odd surprises the yarn might contain. It was often better to have two people working together on a wub like that, as it was very discouraging to tackle on your own!

Good light was very important when picking, or warping, tweed, and the light thoughout the picking shed was always good, from the roof windows. An artist's studio could have done no better. Stepping into the picking shed, you were always aware of two things: the amount of light and that tweed smell!

Left to right: Jamie Hutchison, Pearl Johnson, Kirkabister, Vidlin, Jean Hall, Houll, Andy Robertson. Probably mid fifties.   Photo courtesy of Betty Sutherland.

Picking shed lasses. L. to R. Betty Johnson, Brungasta, Joann Johnson, Ness, Weathersta, (warper), Daisy Anderson, Gonfirth, Hazel Robertson, Isles Road, Jean Hall. Mid fifties.

Photo courtesy of Hazel Hutchison.

Everest and All That

For the knitwear side of the business, there was no push to find jobs for former employees after the war. Its workers were all female, and some were always leaving to get married – which happened a fair bit in the post-war years! At slacker moments, there was no need to recruit replacements. When business picked up new lasses would be taken on and departing employees encouraged to take home jumpers to finish, or take a machine and continue to knit at home. As knitwear was all on piece rates this was quite a popular thing to do.

There were three main work areas in Number Eleven.

(1) The machine-room, nearest the road and facing the Hillend. The machine room had windows, but mostly of frosted glass. Looking out, apparently, was not to be encouraged! (Perhaps you might slip a loop?)

Anna Thomason, Tua, Vidlin in foreground, Maggie Herculeson, Newhouse, Skelberry, behind.
© Shetland Museum.

(2) The finishing end, which was the corner room. Here the ribbed necks and cuffs which were machine-knitted, but in long continuous strips, were sewn (grafted) on to the separately-knitted jumpers. This was "finishing", although it was not actually the last step in the production process. With two sizeable windows this room was light and contained the stove. (Every employee in Number Eleven took a turn at stoking the fire, a week at a time.)

Finishers. Left, Maria Georgeson, Sweening, then Florence Leask, Lee, Gonfirth.
© Shetland Museum.

(3) Inbye, in the biggest room. Inbye was where yarn and garments were despatched to homeworkers, and examining, labelling and later, brushing, were done. This room overlooked the voe and the pier and was quite a lightsome place to work. There was very often a fair bit of activity at the Voe pier, especially in the forties and fifties, what with fishing boats coming and going, and landing their catches.

And you might get a laugh at what you saw, as everybody did the day that a certain Adie's employee was sent to tar the pier and started from the landward side. When he got to the far end he had to be rescued by boat!

Examining was an important part of quality control. Mistakes in machining would never get as far as this final stage; what you were looking at was the quality of the finishing. It had to be done neatly and accurately so that it was unnoticeable. No split loops, squint cuff seams, funny-looking back necks, etc. etc!

Examiners needed good light and good eyesight and so did finishers. Everybody dreaded black jumpers. Many a home finisher's heart sank when a new box of finishing arrived with yet more of them. You would try to complete them in daylight if possible, or bright electric light – if you had it. One poor woman trying to finish black jumpers was caught out when a light bulb fused. The only replacement bulb she had was fairly dim – something like fifteen watts. She drew her chair directly underneath it and soldiered on. It was no use. Not to be beat, she dragged the kitchen table into the middle of the floor, planted her chair on it, climbed up and sat on the chair, as close to the light as she could get!

Finishing (or grafting) was featured in a Voe concert song in the fifties. Written to the tune of "Music, Music, Music", some of it went like this:

> Here we sit an here we stay,
> Sprettin, shewin, makkin tay,
> Busy wirkin everyday,
> Graftin, graftin, graftin.
> I'm dat blyde I'm no a nurse.
> Wirkin nights wid be a curse.
> Heth, you ken, life might be worse
> As graftin, graftin, graftin.
>
> Graftin! Forever graftin!
> Du taks two fae here an two fae dere,
> Every two an two's a pair.
> We just wirk fae nine till six

Sprettin loops an takkin sticks,
Tellin yarns an playin tricks
An graftin, graftin, graftin!

Mimie Scollay (later Pearson), of Braeside, started work in the machine room in December 1948. Anna Thomason (later Johnson) of Tua, Vidlin, had been taken on earlier that year, as had Babsy Hutchison of Hillend (later Anderson) The three lasses were about the same age, not long out of school.

Conversation in the office:

Miss Adie: How old is Mimie Scollay?

Jamie Couper: I tink she's sixteen.

Miss Adie (sighing): Another child!

Number Eleven was never to be as busy again as it was in the thirties, but nevertheless, during the fifties, work was fairly steady. Occasionally there was even overtime. There would be seven machinists or so in the machine room, with two or three folk inbye, and maybe four or five in the finishing end. This, together with a couple of outworker machinists and a varying number of finishers, say about fifteen, made up the knitwear workforce.

In June 1953, while Britain was gearing up for the Queen's coronation, (and tractor-loads of bonfire material were being hauled to the top of the Clubb o Mulla), news came that Mount Everest had been climbed for the first time, by Edmund Hillary and Sherpa Tensing. Voe folk were naturally interested in this great event but even more so as the Everest expedition members, Edmund Hillary included, were wearing jumpers which had been made in Voe.

The publicity arising from this could only be a boon for Adie's, and "Everest" jumpers were requested by customers for years to come. They were not the average kind of jumper, and not, as you might expect, thick and heavy.

The order had come through a regular London customer for jumpers to supply the expedition. The yarn was specially spun in Hawick from Shetland wool. Intended to give warmth without weight, it was a very fine yarn, termed "42 cut", and claimed to be finer than some lace yarns. A 38" jumper weighed only five ounces and a 44" six and a half. They were loosely knitted in oiled yarn, several sizes too big, then washed and shrunk, when they turned out really soft. First Everests were made in natural Shetland colours, but later they were dyed charcoal, Fair Isle red, tartan green and navy.

The most famous Everest customer, after Hillary and Tensing themselves, was probably the singer Adam Faith, who apparently ordered a slipover once.

Mrs Bennett, daughter of James Adie, was now in charge of Number Eleven, and took the staff to Lerwick to see the film about the Everest expedition. The whole episode was a great source of pride to everybody and a huge photo of Hillary and Tensing was prominently displayed for many years.

Hillary and Tensing, 1953. © *BBC.*

Myra Thomason, Tua, Vidlin, who was to become a long-serving member of staff, started work in June 1954. (Myra and Anna Thomason were the daughters of Dolly Brown, the first Voe machinist.) Myra's first job was winding pirms, making tea and sweeping up, but she soon moved on to join Babsy Hutchison inbye where they checked the quality of the finished garments and labelled them before they left the premises.

Like the tweed, knitwear went all over the country and beyond. Some was for Macey's in New York, also Brooks Brothers. You had to put Brooks Brothers labels straight on to the garments, with no Adie's labels. There were orders for Italy and Switzerland, for Bond Street and Highland Home

Industries, for Chalmers of Oban, and many more. And there were special orders for one-off items, such as "da Hong Kong man's cardigan", spoken about for many a day because of the huge size!

Adie's had an agent in London. Samples of new lines would go to this agent for promotion purposes. Myra remembers them coming back at the season's end in need of a good wash.

Publicity materials from the 1950s included these attractive photos of two young lasses then working at Adie's. The location was apparently the old *Sunbeam*, tied up at the Voe pier.

Hazel Robertson (Hutchison).
Courtesy of Hazel Hutchison

Eileen Georgeson.
Courtesy of Eileen Georgeson

Anidder special order:

Characters:
Peter Johnson, Brungasta, shop manager.
Mrs Esme Bennett, manager of Number 11
Myra Thomason
A tourist.

P.J.: (coming into Number Eleven) Mrs Bennett? Are you dere?

E.B.: (emerging from office) Yes, Peter? What is it?

P.J.: Well, der a tourist lady in da shop, an she's needin a jumper made, a special order. I said I wid ax you.

E.B.: Oh, I'm sure we can do that. Myra, I wonder if you could go and get the details? Take a tape measure and get her size.

P.J. to M. T. (on the way to the shop) Wait du for du sees her. She's huge! Du'll never reck aroond her! Yon's her, ida fur cott.

Myra enters shop, brandishing tape measure...

E.B. (as Myra returns) Well, what is it she wants?

M.T.: A 58, wi short airms, an langer ida front as da back.

E.B.: Well, that certainly is a special!

A group of Number Eleven and picking-shed staff, mid fifties. L. to R., Maggie Herculeson, Skelberry, Peggy Hall, Houll, Eileen Georgeson, Skelberry, Joey Sutherland, Orgill, Vidlin, Jeanette Georgeson, Skelberry, Pearl Johnson, Kirkabister, Jean Hall, Houll. In front is Myra Thomason, Tua. Pearl and Jean both picking-shed staff. Photo courtesy of Betty Sutherland.

The all-female atmosphere of Number Eleven changed in the late fifties when Magnus Thompson, Setter, and Gordon Johnson, Kirkabister, Vidlin, were transferred from tweed into the machine room. They would be the first of several male machinists. As we've seen, Pete Blance also came across the road to the knitwear side about this time. Number Eleven always had the reputation of being a lightsome place to work and the men made it no less so!

Pete was to divide his time between the scouring-house and the Number Eleven brushing-machine, which by now was often being used as a final process for jumpers. Brushed jumpers were very popular, and brushing certainly gave a lovely, soft, fluffy appearance to a garment, though old hands felt that it was done to disguise a poorer quality of yarn.

Fourteen to Five

Scouring tweed and washing hosiery, which had been done for many years in Fourteen, moved to new premises shortly after the war, possibly about 1947. The new scouring-house was at the top of the pier, the building which now belongs to Olnafirth Sea Farm.

The end section of this building, Number Five, nearest to the pier, was specially built for a tweed-washing machine which actually had to be sunk into the floor. There were two massive wooden rollers, one driven by a 7 h.p. Petter diesel engine. Two wubs of tweed would be sewn together end-to-end for washing and the machine would wash four wubs at one time. Round and round they would go through the big rollers, through soda, through soap flakes and through rinsing water. Stop the machine, undo the raeping string, run out the wubs and hank them out into a basket.

Looking down the Voe pier, late fifties. Scouring-house on left. Boat at pier is Sunbeam LK 453 (ex Kate LK 126).
© Shetland Museum

The next step was the "hydro-extractor", a kind of big spin-drier, which could take two wubs at a time. This, too, was belt-driven by the same engine. You had to be "braaly parteeklar" when loading the extractor, and load it evenly. There was a story told of a similar machine in the Borders somewhere that had not been loaded evenly. Apparently, it wobbled, the drum hit the (quarter-inch thick) casing and it came right out through the wall!

Finally, the wubs were carried upstairs into Number Six next door and hung on battens

Jamie Johnson. © Bowie.
Photo courtesy of Bella Hughson.

to dry. All this was a tremendous step forward from hand-washing tweed!

The upstairs floor was covered with zig-zagging heating pipes. The hot water came directly from a coal-fired stove downstairs in Number Seven. There was another stove to heat the water for washing.

Washing and drying tweed, even with a machine, was really a two-person job. The best-known team seem to have been Andy Robertson and Jamie Johnson, Garths. They were a lightsome pair who specialised in composing topical verses, and Jamie, apparently, would often burst into song!

Peggy Parkin continued to wash tweed after the war, often with Robbie Hall, Muckle Roe. She also washed hosiery, all still by hand, and when she left, Tina Anderson of Hoga carried on, from 1955 to 1958, followed by Pete Blance. Other people also did washing at various times. Jumpers were washed downstairs in Number Five and then boarded and dried upstairs, like the tweed. By 1956, there was mains electricity and, thank goodness, a washing machine!

Tina Anderson (Johnson). Tina had also worked as a maid in Skol for a time. Courtesy of Tina Johnson.

Pete Blance washing jumpers.
Photo © Dennis Coutts, courtesy of Pete Blance.

Emigrants

At various times there have been waves of emigration from Shetland. The fifties were one of those times. Some slipped away across the globe without much trace; others seemed to retain family and community ties almost as strong as if they had never left.

Archie Johnson of Hillcrest, excellent joiner that he was, took his skills and his family to Australia in 1954. The whole community at the time felt their departure. The family kept very much in touch with Shetland, and over the years, many visits have been paid in both directions.

Katie and Archie Johnson with three of their family of five, Grace, Hakki (James) and Mary.

Bella Johnson of Kurkigarth, who used to be cook in Voe House, married Tom Coutts from Scalloway, and, after living in London for a short time, returned to Shetland to say goodbye before emigating to New Zealand in 1957.

Bobby Anderson of the Hoga wove tweed at Voe till he did his National Service, then was back again until tweed grew slacker in the late fifties. Bobby did electrical wiring at the time of the coming of mains electricity, and then set out for New Zealand in 1959, as the Murray boys of Weathersta had already done.

As years went by, Bobby was back home on several occasions, and just as much part of the place as he always was. The first time, he told his

Bobby Anderson.
Photo courtesy of Tina Johnson.

family not to say he was coming, he would just like to arrive at Voe "just as da folk is aa comin oot for der denner!" They had to tell him that it had changed somewhat!

Outside wark

Plans had been drawn up for another house at Burnside and the windows for it had actually been made, by Archie Johnson, before he emigrated in 1954. The house was never built and the windows were put into storage. However, until the slump in the tweed in the late fifties, there was plenty of outside work going on at Voe. In 1957, there was still a carpenter squad of four men: John Wood of Sullom, Willie Couper, Seaview, Mac Brown and Attie Thompson. Their work was very varied; they did repairs and maintenance to all the buildings, they helped Joseph Cheyne on the farm, they cut and cured peats for Bellevue, Voe House and the business, and even lighted all the fires.

Tea, Tourists and Toilets

The upper floor of the shop, which in pre-war days had held clothes for sale, had by the late fifties developed into a showroom for tweed and knitwear. Hand-knits and other locally-produced items, e.g. sheepskins, were bought in and shown here too. The aim was to sell to the tourist market and pretty good trade was often done. Bus tours brought tourists regularly to Voe and teas were laid on for the visitors in one of the side rooms upstairs. There was, it is remembered, "a fair bizz on when da buses cam."

Tea was very much appreciated by the tourist parties. Their other priority was, of course, toilets. Now, toilets had never been a first priority in Voe (or any other place at that time, probably!). Staff away back in the old days had "held in" till dinner-time or tea-time. There are horror stories about the state of a certain burn… There were toilets over this burn, and also in da ebb at various times, but eventually, as hygiene standards improved, inside toilets did appear, in pretty out of the way corners like behind the warping-shed. And the Number Eleven basement, where tourists were usually directed. This toilet, in later years, was reached through an outside door at basement level, but for a good while, needful tourists had to go through the knitwear department and downstairs.

Inbye staff in Number Eleven grew quite used to processions of folk trooping in and out through their work area. Cheerful, apologetic, inquisitive, chatty, snooty, wet, dry or in between, they all climbed down and up the wooden stair whether they were nineteen or ninety, walking sticks and all. How things change!

Dances and Romances

There seem to have been two "Employees' dances": at least, two that are still remembered, one sometime in the thirties and one about 1950/ 51.
   In the 30s:

> "Oh, it wis greatly lookit forward tae. Da lasses in Brungasta spak aboot it in weeks!"
>
> "I mind Mammie's dress yet."
>
> "Yea, it wis a dressy affair. Du sees, da Adies wis dere, an dey set da standard!"
>
> "It wis da employees dance, an dey *invited* da Adies."
>
> "Dey hed tea, sandwiches, an fancies fae da bakery. An everybody took a pairtner. It wis a right good night."

There was even a poem. Willie Irvine, one of the Scalloway weavers, who was later to marry Mina Robertson of Quam, wrote *"The Hall by the Sea"*, after this dance. He describes a company from a wide area – Bixter, Aith, Vidlin, Mossbank, etc. Supper tables were set, for twenty couples at a time, the food was good and *"… you can get something far stronger than tea."* The dancing seems to have been hearty:

> There were foxtrots and Bostons and waltzes and all
> And four Shetland reels which near did for the hall
> For with backsteps, and frontsteps, and steps to the side
> Twas a noise like you'd hear in a yard on the Clyde.

About 1950:
A staff do was again organised by a group of employees and management were invited. Again, everybody could take a partner, and again, it was a great success. But it was the new Voe Hall this time, up at Isles Road, and the food, like the hall, had moved on a bit. It was roast beef and tatties for all and it was the first sit-down, fork-and-knife meal ever held in the new hall.

The beef was roasted in the bakery oven, looked after by Danny Leask, one of the bakers, and Bob Hamilton, Ted Adie's nephew, then one of the managers at Voe. It was to be served cold but when it arrived at the hall to be sliced up nobody was anxious to take on this important job. A piece of beef as substantial as this had not been seen in a long time. Said Geordie Duncan of Collafirth, "Give me da knife, I'll slice it!" Nobody thought this a very great idea, as Geordie had sometimes been considered a bit handless – but somebody passed him the knife. They had surely all forgotten that Geordie had spent his war service in the Army Catering Corps! He made a beautiful job of slicing the beef and everybody was most impressed! Bob Hamilton gave him a special mention in a speech later on in the night.

"An what aboot romances?" "Oh, dey were nae want o dem!"

The number of married couples who met at Voe, or both worked at Voe, over all the years, must run into scores, if not treble figures. Add to that a good number of more short-lived courtships and the many "notions" that were cherished, some recognised, some secret, and you can see that this peerie cluster of buildings was pretty much a hotbed of romance!

What else could it be? So many folk there, and so many of them young folk, from different areas. In its heyday, Adie's was a great place to meet people.

It was unlikely, (though it did happen !) that the pair of you would actually be working in the same department. In fact, you were not likely to see each other all that often during the day, as there was very little coming and going between departments except on business. But there was twal time and denner time, and in the case of the bakers, breakfast time, when you might get a glimpse of him or her, or a word or two, or even a chance to sit together, or walk back from your denner together. There was the shop, where you might just bump into somebody, say, when you were collecting your errands at night on the way to the van. And there was the van run itself, of course, which could be pretty lively sometimes, sitting in semi-darkness, lurching around corners, sliding along the wooden seats, and always somebody just ready to torment or play tricks on you…

Most importantly, there was the grapevine, always buzzing, keeping you informed as to what social events were on in the district, and not only that, but who was likely to be there. The grapevine also made it difficult to keep anything quiet, and almost impossible to keep a new relationship secret. You just had to resign yourself to a lot of teasing!

High Days and Holidays

Come you fae Mossbank, come you fae Brae,
Come ower da hills fae Dury Voe,

> Come you wi your coo, we'll be blyde ta see you,
> Come ta da Voe roup on Friday-o.
>
> *(from a song written in the early sixties)*

In actual fact, the Voe Roup day was usually a Thursday. It happened twice a year, once in May and once in October. In the days when every croft had at least one cow, a cattle sale was a big and important event, involving a great many people from Voe and the surrounding areas, and attended by cattle buyers, both local and from south. It was an all-day affair until later years. And Adie's marked it by declaring a holiday, except for the office, the shop and the bakery despatch room. The bakers themselves would start and therefore finish work a bit earlier than usual.

The system was this, at least in the post-war years, and probably before that as well. If you had an animal to sell, you let Adie's office know, and it got put on the sale list. The sale was organised, advertised, the auctioneer booked and on the roup day you headed along to the roup green, with your cow, quaig, stot, calves or whatever you had, all on tethers, and using whatever transport you could get. Very likely you just walked, unless you lived pretty far away, in which case you might get together with some of your neighbours and hire a truck, e.g. from Sursetter or Erty Jamieson of Southerhouse.

The roup green was down at Voe. The present-day house of Solglint was built on the site. On a roup day, it was a scene of tremendous activity, not to say noise! Magnie Anderson of Hoga was often the one who called out the order of sale, as he had a fine loud voice!

And so it went on, all day. Sales were made, and buyers paid in cash. When your cow was sold, you were given a chit which you took down to Adie's office, and you were given cash, which amounted to the price of your cow less a commission fee which paid the auctioneer,etc. And there it was, real money. You might just feel like stepping into the shop next door and buying yourself something. Like a dram, maybe.

The roup day was a big day socially for many years. There were so many people about, going to the roup with kye, waiting their turn at the sale ring, coming from the office with money, spending the day as there was no instant transport home. People went shopping and visiting, stood about yarning, bought themselves food. Rows of women would be seen walking out and in the road, with linked arms. Tea used to be available at Number Fourteen, served through the top half of the stable-style door. (Tea, and in later years, coffee were always provided at the roup green for the auctioneer and buyers. These refreshments would be brought down by the maids from Voe House or Bellevue.)

There was always plenty of stronger refreshment on the roup day! Bairns coming home from school would feel a bit wary sometimes of what they might come upon. "Dey were aye drunks aboot!"

It was rather a difficult situation if one of the "drunks" was a buyer, not a seller! This did regularly happen in one case at least, and obliging neighbours and friends would have to round up kye at the end of the day and get them and their new owner safely home to house and byre. Eventually, someone challenged him. "Man, du'll hae ta gie dis up. Du's comin ower aald for dis kerry-on noo." "Weel," he replied, "du sees, I'm classed as a baess-buyer, an if du's a baess-buyer, du haes ta buy kye!"

It was quite a day. "Yes, he wis some day, da roup day!"

And what about the night? Well, there would often have been a dance. There was an old saying too: "As hot as love on a roup night!"

By the time the song was written, the roup had ceased to be such an important event. Fewer and fewer people had kye to sell. It shrank to a half-day, then smaller still, and Adie's stopped taking the holiday. The odd dram might still be exchanged at the Sparl Road gate but the high days were over!

The Queen's Visit

Extract from *The Shetland Times*, Friday 12th August, 1960:

> ... again informality was the keynote. Royalty mingled with commoner with the greatest of ease. There was no shoving, and everyone got a good view of the visitors as they visited three sections of Messrs T.M. Adie's premises - the hosiery department, the weaving shed, and the finishing shed.
>
> In the hosiery department, Mrs Mary Hutchison, one of the oldest

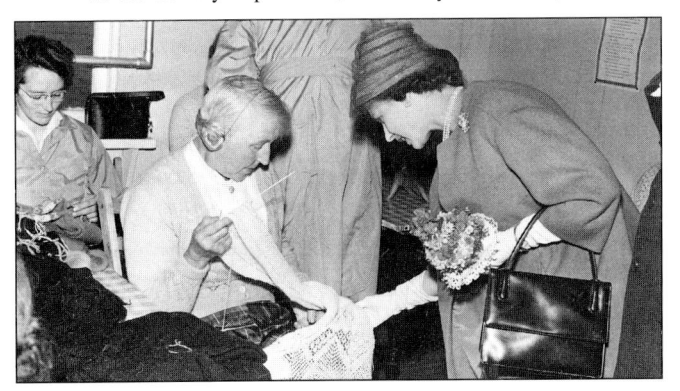

Mary Hutchison (Tulloch), of Hillside, with the Queen. Back left is Aggie Blance, Gonfirth. © Dennis Coutts.

employees, was knitting a shawl from fine lace yarn. The Queen admired the fine quality of the yarn, and the Duke cracked a joke about her ablity to knit without looking.

In the department was the oldest lady the royal pair met during their tour - Mrs Catherine Robertson, of Collafirth, who is 91 years of age. Mrs Robertson had been in some doubt about her ability to attend, but she was driven from her home to Voe, and was really charmed by the Queen and Duke.

In the weaving shed, Major E.P.Adie showed the guests around, and explained the working of the looms. There are six men working in the shed at the moment , and the Queen spoke to one of them, Mr George Johnson. It was a rather unfortunate moment for Mr Johnson - just as the Queen approached he got a "broken shot" (the thread broke) and he had to start to repair the damage under a royal eye. The Queen noted with a sympathetic look that something was wrong. As Mr Johnson said later, he can work all day without anything like that happening - and it had to happen to him at that particular moment.

In the finishing department, the Duke spoke to two local girls, Betty Johnson and Jean Hall. The girls were greatly pleased by the interest shown by the visitors.

On left, Betty Johnson, Brungasta, then Jean Hall, Houll. At the back, working on a hanging wub, is Johnny Hughson. Major Adie far right. © **Dennis Coutts.**

The Queen and the Duke were shown patterns of Shetland tweed, and asked to make a choice, so that the employees could present them with lengths. But time was short and the choice so difficult that the Queen asked if the patterns could be sent to her, so that she could choose at leisure. This will be done.

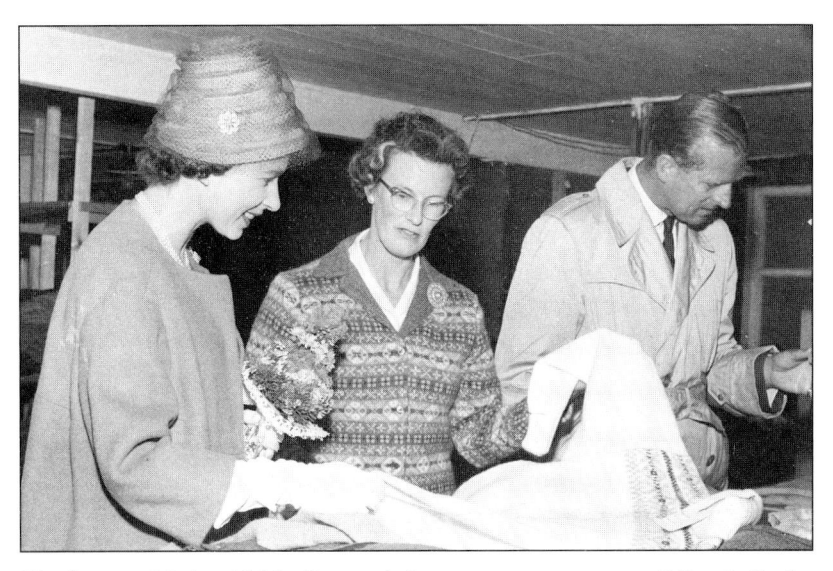

The Queen and Duke with Mrs Bennett, knitwear manager. © **Dennis Coutts.**

It was a Wednesday. *The Shetland Times* thought the Queen rather lightly-clad for "one of the worst days of the summer", with showers and a wind speed of 25 knots gusting to 40. All this after six weeks of good weather.

It didn't matter. None of it mattered. We didn't have TV at that time. We felt pretty distant from the mainland of Britain. The Queen had never visited Shetland before; nor had any monarch for seven hundred years. We had seen her on newsreel films, but apart from that, we'd only seen her photograph, or prints of paintings, like the one on the school wall. There were folk who didn't care that much for royalty but it was a rare person who was not interested. The bairns were off school, clutching their flags and all keyed up with excitement. It really was a big day. Folk were genuinely thrilled.

And there she was. "Such a peerie body". "Awful thin - legs laek sticks!" "So yon's her, poor ting." "Very plaesant-laek, an sae is he."

She was dressed in cyclamen, according to *The Shetland Times*. Everybody thought it was pink.

Nobody ever forgot.

Some moments from the day

In the doorway of the picking shed, Andy Robertson and Johnny Hughson, both former Navy men, stood surveying the strings of flags being hung up. "Boy, dis is signal flags, can du mind what dey staand for noo?" "Deevil een o me can mind da half o dem." The men with the ladders came into earshot. "Boys, you'll hae ta watch foo you hing dis flags up. Every wan o dem staands for a letter o da alphabet, an you ken, Philip is a Navy man, he'll be able ta understaand what you're sayin!" The nearest flag-hanger began to look worried. "Weel, what does dis say, dan?" "Oh na yon's aa right, yon's V - I - M. He'll just tink it's an advert!"

In Number Eleven, all the employees and some home knitters were sitting in their places in good time ready for "inspection". Maggie Grains, (the former Maggie Sutherland), had also come to Voe in good time to see the Queen and nipped in to Number Eleven to see any of her old workmates that were there. She spied Jessie Johnson of Muckle Roe, and made her way in by to speak. Her high heels caught on a bar of wood on the floor and she landed right on top of Jessie. Maggie burst out laughing and picked herself up, saying "Weel, I hoop da Duke o Edinburgh doesna dö da sam ta dee!"

Old lady, after the press cameras had gone: "Bairns, did you see da lightning?"

Edward P. Adie (Ted)
1890-1977

Edward Adie was the youngest of a family of eleven. He was married to Dorothy (Dolla) Anderson of Hillswick, and their home was Bellevue. They had no children.

His obituary in *The Shetland Times* speaks of the public figure: the First World War veteran with the M.C., the emigrant to Canada who returned to take up the family business, the wartime Home Defence man, the County Councillor, Convenor and Deputy Lord Lieutenant, the excellent committee chairman. "From the chair", says the

Edward P. Adie.
Photo courtesy of James A. Adie

Times, "he spoke very little himself, but when he spoke everybody listened." Nobody in Voe would have been surprised to hear that!

He was a tall man with a rather gruff manner, and not talkative by nature; he was not given to making idle conversation with his employees, and tended rather to keep a distance. Few staff were aware of his sense of humour. But he was very largely liked as a boss; he was considered a fair and kindly man, with a very good head for business. He is credited with much of the success of the firm from the twenties onwards. Outwith the firm, he was the local councillor for many years, and always supported the community, often in a quiet way. The Sunday School picnic organiser, for example, might arrive at the shop to find the bills already paid. For the first bairns' Christmas party after the war, when fruit had hardly been seen in years, he procured and donated apples. He played an important part in the building of the new Voe hall in the late forties, a similar role when the new kirk was built, and he continued to support local events throughout his life.

No more Adie's biscuits

After the tremendous demands of the war years, the bakery had to settle back a bit, but it remained busy. In summer 1957 these were the bakery staff:

Ian Johnson, Brae	(despatch room)
Tammy Hall, Muckle Roe	(despatch room)
Lowrie Brown, Isles Road	
Andy Couper, Burnside	
Danny Leask from Lerwick, who lived in Brungasta	
Johnny Johnson, Bankhaven, Hillend	
Joe Robertson, Isles Road	
Harold Johnson, Bayview, Brae	
Zander Hughson, Hillcrest	
Jim Couper, Seaview	

Maurice Hughson joined the bakery staff about 1962 and started in the despatch room with Ian Johnson. At this time, the bakery had the services of two van drivers – Gideon Hall and Tammy Hughson, Maurice's uncle. Tammy drove solely for the bakery.

There had been one or two changes since 1957: Tammy Hall, Danny Leask, and Andy Couper had left. Victor Johnson, Pund, Dale, John Johnson of Isles Road, and Douglas Wood had arrived. Douglas, youngest son of van driver John

Douglas Wood.
Photo courtesy of Diane Wood.

Wood, had started work in Voe, but had then been a baker in Edinburgh.

When Maurice began to train as a baker, production was roughly this:
- 20-odd dozen rolls a day
- More plain buns than rolls
- Mostly plain loaf, biscuits and oatcakes:
- 240 loaf a day
- Only 2 days pan loaf
- (7 bolls of flour used for biscuits)
- 10-20 dozen bannocks a day
- 10 dozen meat pies on a big day
- Very few fancies
- "Twopenny scones" were a good seller. (Even then they cost a lot more than twopence!)

In the bakery, late 1950s. L. to R., Danny Leask, Brungasta, Harold Johnson, Bayview, Brae, Zander Hughson, Hillcrest.   © Shetland Museum.

In 1964, the bakery business was taken over by the bakers themselves, and became known as "Johnson and Wood", the names of the principal bakers and shareholders, Johnny Johnson and Douglas Wood. The name remains to this day.

It has always been a busy place. As the equipment has increased and bakeries in Shetland have grown fewer, bakers' hours have grown longer.

Now, at the turn of the century, production runs like this:
- 200 dozen rolls a day (it can be many more)
- A lot less loaf and biscuits.
- 160 loaf a day
- Many more brown and wholemeal loaf made now
- (A boll and a half flour used for biscuits per week)
- 60 - 100 dozen bannocks a day
- (800doz. bannocks made for New Year 2000!)
- Rather less than half as many oatcakes
- 40 dozen mixed kinds of pies on an average day

Comparing these figures to the 1960s, everybody will have their own theories!

Some other facts

In the old days, flour came off the steamer in 280 lb sacks, was wheeled up

Maurice Hughson, 1998.

Willie Robertson, 1998.

Despatch room staff, 1998: from left, Agnes Anne Laurenson, Anne Marie Jamieson, Harriet Wishart, Lilian Robertson.

from the pier on a handbarrow (and surely handled by more than one man?) Then it came in 140 lb sacks. Then 112 lb. Now the bags weigh 70 lb or 35 kilos, which is supposed to be the limit that any person should lift! (The main flour they use, of course, comes by tanker and is stored in a silo.)

When we joined the EEC, the flour changed. Before that, it was all Canadian flour, now it's EEC flour. And yes, it does taste different.

Did the bakery profit from the oil boom? Well, it was good in a way, because of the great demand for bread, but difficult in another way. They could have sold ten times the amount but could not get the staff to do it. Bakers in other parts of Shetland were able to recruit women. There was plenty of work for Delting women!

The bakers always used to work on Christmas morning and New Year's morning. (Quite sociable occasions they were, too). They did have the day after free!

Photos show bakery staff in 1998.

Laurence Thompson and Ian Taylor, 1998.   Sam Eldridge, 1998.

The Later Years

From the sixties onwards, as the bakery developed and went its own way, the rest of the business continued, on a gradually reducing scale

Miss Adie died in February, 1965, at the age of 93. She had lived on her own, apart from her maid, for a few years. (The last maid in Voe House was Tina Wood, Parkgate.) Voe House was sold in 1966 to Lt-Col and Mrs Charles Durham, who ran it for a time as a successful private hotel. (It now belongs to B.P.)

Number 11 staff, 1968. Standing, from left, Helen Wood, Parkgate; Annabel Cheyne, Newhouse; Myra Thomason. Sitting, Peter Wood, Parkgate; Margaret Robertson, Wirlie, Vidlin; Pete Blance; Wilma Hutchison, Hillend; Arnold Gear, Nesting; Maurice Thompson, Nesting. Machine room staff were Annabel, Peter, Margaret, Arnold and Maurice.

In knitwear, there were now such things as a linking machine and Fair Isle knitting machines. The photograph opposite shows the Number Eleven staff, one sunny dinner-hour in July 1968. Out of the nine, five were machinists. There still continued to be quite a few home-finishers and knitters.

The shop continued to be busy for a long time. When Pete Blance's wife, Kathleen, joined the staff in 1970, Peter Hughson was then shop manager. Peter had been in the shop all his working life, apart from the war years, and would remain until his retirement in 1983. The other assistants were Leonard Anderson, Gruttin, and John Thompson (now of Litlatoo). Peter Johnson of

Leonard Anderson, Gruttin, in the 1980s. **Photo courtesy of John Sutherland.**

Peter Hughson, shop manager, who retired in 1983.
Photo courtesy of Bella Hughson.

Joseph Cheyne, who retired from the farm in 1974.
Photo courtesy of Leonard Cheyne.

Jamie and Maggie Ann Couper. Jamie worked at Voe for fifty years, first in the despatch room, then in the office, and Maggie Ann (Williamson), was in Number Eleven for sixteen years.
© Dennis Coutts.

Hillside would work in the summer holidays. (Back in the twenties, Peter's grandfather, another Peter Johnson of Hillside, had worked in the Voe shop too.)

Even in the seventies, beer was still being bottled in the back shop.

Joseph Cheyne retired from the farm in 1974, and Jamie Couper from the office in 1975.

The post office returned to Voe in 1978, after fifty years at the Tagon shop. It was established in part of the main office.

The late sixties and early seventies saw quite a boom in employment in Shetland. A much bigger boom followed, of course, in the late 1970s, when Sullom Voe and B.P. began to dominate the scene. By 1981, Adie's were down to ten employees in total. Three of these were still employed in tweed.

The last weaver in Voe was Bert Manson, Pund; his father Magnie had retired in 1982. Magnie Manson had been at Adie's since 1928.

Anne and James A. Adie at shop door.
Photo courtesy James A. Adie.

The last of the Number Eleven staff were Myra Thomason, Helen Thompson, (formerly Wood), Litlatoo, and Peter Wood of Parkgate, the last machinist. Number Eleven itself actually closed its doors in 1988, and the staff transferred to the re-arranged Picking Shed. They took the number "11" with them to the door of their new base. Myra left in 1990, having been at Voe since 1954. Tweed and hosiery came quietly to an end, with stock being sold off in December 1991.

An what cam o da place?

The picking shed was sold to Keith Robertson, who turned it into a dwelling-house, and retained the name "The Picking Shed". The weaving shed and Number Fourteen were sold to Allan Johnson, son of Dodie and Mary Johnson. The weaving shed became a joinery workshop and Fourteen a store. The scouring house and drying loft building (Numbers 5, 6 and 7) now belongs to Olnafirth Sea Farm. Interestingly, while all these buildings were being renovated in the 1990s, some beautifully made windows came out of storage and were at last used. Archie Johnson had made them in the early fifties, before he left for Australia!

Old Number Eleven became the property of the Shetland Amenity Trust, was turned into a camping böd, and is now known once again as the Sail Loft!

The shop was sold in 1991 to Alex Couper, son of Jamie and Maggie Ann Couper. It was sold on at New Year 1995 to Clive Mowat and Margaret Kirk, and became the Pierhead Bar and Restaurant.

The bakery continues to be very busy.

The Voe pier has recently been taken over by the Voe Pier Trust, who have plans to replace it and improve facilities.

And so Adie's has passed into history, with all its ups and downs, hard work and hilarity.

"Wark? Yes, yes, wark, when dey were very little wark ta be hed!"

"Everybody at wanted got wark, an a start in life, even if dey didna bide lang."

"Dey were a real community feeling, wi all dat long-term staff."

"Characters? Man, da place wis full o characters!"

"Oh, bairns, we hed mony a fun. Does du no mind da day......?"

To say that Adie's was important to the area is a great understatement. There were local evictions and much poverty in the nineteenth century; in the first half of the twentieth, that poverty continued, there were two world wars and a national Depression. Nobody ever got rich from working at Adie's, but it gave a great stability to the place for many years. It is the reason why many of us live where we live now, the reason why many couples met and married, and why Voe survived so well as a community through more than one set of hard times.

From da Yarn Store

There is a great store of stories about life and incidents at Voe.

Jookery-packery

The work done at Adie's was skilled, painstaking, and by its nature, repetitive. It could have been, and sometimes it was, boring. But few days went by without diversion of some kind. There was gossip, and jokes, and yarns, sometimes poetry, and tales of the latest remarks and exploits of one or other of the characters of the place.

And... there was flour in the bakery, water in the scouring-house, soot on the doors of the old stoves, fish at the pier. Plenty of scope for the practical joker, and Voe seems to have been a great place for practical jokes! It was, for example, very unwise to leave footwear unattended. You might find anything in a pair of boots, anything, from a dead sillock to a live mouse. Your weaving-shed smucks might even be nailed fast to the floor! And there you would be, part of a story, just like the rest...

Number 1 Reception:

Before the days of public halls, which probably means before the First World War, the old meal store, Number 1, was sometimes used for wedding celebrations. One particular wedding held there was remembered because of the unusual circumstances. The marriage had not been able to take place as the banns had not been properly called; however, since everything was organised for the reception, the foy went ahead.

It is said that, after the reception, half the wedding company followed the couple home to see what would happen next! On arriving home, the groom declared *"Weel, I tink I'll geng oot an maa!"* And he proceeded to do so!

Child care in the early 20th century:

Mrs Hanka Adie happened one day to meet Willie Brown of Kirkhouse, whose infant son, Johnny, was about the same age as her own baby. She stopped to ask after the family, "and has the baby been out yet?" "He, he!" was the reply, "he'll never be oot till he walks oot himsell!"

Crime and punishment:

A certain man in the neighbourhood (goodness knows when!) became convinced that somebody was stealing his peats. His peat stack stood near the road and so was quite accessible. Time went on and the peat stack continued to shrink rather too fast, so eventually, as he could not discover who was to blame, he resorted to drastic measures. He doctored a peat with gunpowder, carefully laid it well to the front of the stack, and waited to see what happened.

The peat disappeared, and very shortly afterwards, one of the van drivers had a request for a rather heavy "sent errand" to Lerwick. Somebody, *(an we dönna ken wha!)* was needing a new top for their stove!

Politics, politics:

Danny Leask, who was a baker at Voe for years, and a leading member of the local concert party, was also a staunch Labour Party man. During one General Election campaign, a Conservative Party poster appeared outside Number Eleven, a big picture of the Tory candidate of the day. Mrs Bennett had just pinned it up before she went home at dinner-time. When she returned, the man had been cut out of the poster and he was hanging by the neck just outside her office door! She was aware of a certain amount of interest from the windows of the bakery opposite!

And finally…

A certain amount of formality existed between staff and management. This rarely weakened, but Magnie Anderson, for one, was in the habit of addressing Bob Hamilton, one of the younger managers, as "Bob". One day, the weavers had been waiting a little beyond the usual time for the shed to be opened, so Magnie set off up to Voe House to see what was happening. "Is Bob in?" says Magnie. He was met with "*Mister* Hamilton has just gone down!" "Oh weel, dat's fine. Aa da idder Mesters is sittin on da daek!"

There are plenty more yarns in the yarn store, if you're interested. Just find somebody who used to work at Voe, and see what they can tell you!

Bibliography

Donaldson, Gordon, *Northwards by Sea,* Paul Harris Publishing, Edinburgh, 1978.

Halcrow, A., *Sail Fishermen of Shetland,* The Shetland Times Ltd., Lerwick, 1994.

Irvine, James W., *The Giving Years,* Shetland Publishing Co., Lerwick, 1991.

Irvine, James W., *The Waves are Free,* Shetland Publishing Co., Lerwick, 1988.

Jamieson, Peter, *Letters on Shetland,* Moray Press, Edinburgh, 1949.

Manson's Almanac